Sex as a Protected Ground in International and Domestic Law

Comparative Discrimination Law

Volumes published in this Brill Research Perspectives title are listed at *brill.com/rpcd*

Sex as a Protected Ground in International and Domestic Law

By

Christine Forster
Vedna Jivan

BRILL

LEIDEN | BOSTON

This paperback book edition is simultaneously published as issue 4.3–4 (2020) of *Comparative Discrimination Law*, DOI:10.1163/24522031-12340010

The Library of Congress Cataloging-in-Publication Data is available online at http://catalog.loc.gov

Typeface for the Latin, Greek, and Cyrillic scripts: "Brill". See and download: brill.com/brill-typeface.

ISBN 978-90-04-34593-5 (paperback)
ISBN 978-90-04-34592-8 (e-book)

This book is printed on acid-free paper and produced in a sustainable manner.

Contents

Sex as a Protected Ground in International and Domestic Law 1
Christine Forster and Vedna Jivan
Abstract 1
Keywords 1
Introduction 2
Part 1: Sex as a Protected Ground 2
1.1 *Our Approach to Comparative Law* 6
1.2 *Organization of This Volume* 9
Part 2: Sex as an Internationally-Protected Ground in Human Rights Law 9
2.1 *International Covenant on Civil and Political Rights 1966* 12
2.2 *International Covenant on Economic, Social and Cultural Rights 1966* 24
2.3 *Convention on the Elimination of All Forms of Discrimination against Women 1979* 27
Part 3: Translating International Sex Discrimination Law into Domestic Law 43
3.1 *The Application of Sex Protection in the United States* 44
3.1.1 Disparate Treatment 46
3.1.1.1 *Opposite-Sex Comparator* 47
3.1.1.2 *'Because of' Sex: Causation* 50
3.1.1.3 *Discrimination Must Be Intentional* 54
3.1.1.4 *Discrimination Must Be against an Individual* 57
3.1.1.5 *Bona Fide Occupational Qualification* 58
3.1.2 Disparate Impact 61
3.2 *The Application of Sex Protection in Australia* 65
3.2.1 Direct Discrimination 66
3.2.1.1 *Opposite-Sex Comparator* 67
3.2.1.2 *'By Reason of' Sex: Causation* 70
3.2.1.3 *Sexual Harassment* 72
3.2.1.4 *Maternity Leave Return* 76
3.2.1.5 *Workplace Culture* 79
3.2.1.6 *Male Plaintiffs* 80
3.2.2 Indirect Discrimination 81
3.3 *The Application of Sex Protection in India* 87
3.3.1 Opposite-Sex Comparator 89
3.3.2 'Only of' Sex: Causation 99

Part 4: Comparing International and Domestic Sex Discrimination Law 106
4.1 *The Scope of 'Sex'* 107
4.2 *The Requirement of an 'Individual' Victim* 109
4.3 *The Requirement of an Opposite-Sex Comparator* 112
4.4 *Indirect Discrimination* 116
4.5 *The Requirement of an Intent to Discriminate* 119
4.6 *Multiple Discrimination* 120
4.7 *Concluding Comments* 123

Sex as a Protected Ground in International and Domestic Law

Christine Forster
University of New South Wales
c.forster@unsw.edu.au

Vedna Jivan
University of New South Wales
v.jivan@unsw.edu.au

Abstract

This volume in the Brill Research Perspectives in Comparative Discrimination Law addresses sex as a protected ground in international and domestic law. It compares sex discrimination protection through three thematic lenses. Firstly, it charts and compares the evolution and development of sex discrimination protection in international human rights law in three treaty-bodies – the CEDAW Committee, the HRC and the CESCR. Secondly, it then takes up the evolution and development of sex discrimination protection in three domestic law frameworks – the United States, Australia and India. Finally, the development of sex discrimination protection in international law is compared with the development of sex discrimination protection in the domestic legal contexts of the three country examples, with the implications of that comparison analysed. This volume seeks to show that despite differences in the way that international approaches to sex discrimination are translated into domestic law and differences in social, political and cultural contexts women face similar limitations in accessing justice through sex discrimination frameworks.

Keywords

comparative law – discrimination – sex – protected grounds – CEDAW – ICCPR – ICESCR – Title VII – intersectionality – multiple discrimination – same-sex comparator – Constitution of India – Australia Sex Discrimination Act

 | DOI:10.1163/9789004345928_002

Introduction

This volume is the tenth in the Brill Research Perspectives series concerning comparative discrimination law. This series addresses comparative discrimination issues both horizontally (overarching frameworks) and vertically (specific issues within discrimination law). Topics include unlawful discrimination on the basis of race, sex, religion, age, disability, gender, sexual orientation, as well as intersectionality – at national, regional, and international levels. Theoretical as well as more pragmatic approaches, such as the use of active measures to combat structural discrimination and proving discrimination claims with empirical evidence, are also explored. Law by its nature is bound by culture and language, and the effort in the series has been made to examine issues of discrimination from different jurisdictions.

This tenth volume in the Brill Research Perspectives in Comparative Discrimination Law addresses sex discrimination protection through three thematic lenses. Firstly, it charts and compares the evolution and development of sex discrimination protection in international human rights law in three treaty-bodies – the CEDAW Committee, the HRC and the CESCR. Secondly, it then takes up the evolution and development of sex discrimination protection in three domestic law frameworks – the United States, Australia and India. Finally, the development of sex discrimination protection in international law is compared with the development of sex discrimination protection in the domestic legal contexts of the three country examples, with the implications of that comparison analysed. This volume seeks to show that despite differences in the way that international approaches to sex discrimination are translated into domestic law and differences in social, political and cultural contexts women face similar limitations in accessing justice through sex discrimination frameworks.

The editors welcome suggestions as to authors and jurisdictions outside those presented in the volumes to date. This series is to run for ten years of quarterly volumes, with the ambition to achieve a broad approach to comparative discrimination law issues.

Part 1: Sex as a Protected Ground

'Sex' traditionally refers to the biological and physiological characteristics that define men and women, for example, their different reproductive systems. As a protected ground of discrimination, sex entered international human rights law with the adoption of the Universal Declaration of Human Rights in 1945, followed by its inclusion in the *International Covenant on Civil and Political Rights* 1966 (*ICCPR*) and the *International Covenant on Economic, Social and Cultural Rights* 1966 (*ICESCR*). The intended meaning and scope of 'sex', however, was undefined in these early human rights conventions. The *Convention on the Elimination of All Forms of Discrimination against Women* 1979 (*CEDAW*), adopted two decades later, provided a more comprehensive definition of sex discrimination to include:

> [A]ny distinction, exclusion or restriction made on the basis of sex which has the effect or purpose of impairing or nullifying the recognition, enjoyment or exercise by women, irrespective of their marital status, on a basis of equality of men and women, of human rights and fundamental freedoms in the political, economic, social, cultural, civil or any other field.[1]

Sex, as a prohibited ground of discrimination, was translated from international human rights law into world constitutions and legislation as different countries ratified or acceded to these human rights conventions and set about meeting their international obligations. 'Sex has evolved in definition, scope and interpretation in both the international law context and in the domestic law context since its first appearance in 1945.

This volume concerns sex as a protected ground of discrimination. It focuses on the meaning of sex, the meaning of sex discrimination, the inclusion of both direct and indirect discrimination, the elements required to establish direct and indirect sex discrimination including (variously) an opposite-sex comparator, causation, intention, an adverse event and finally the applicability of any defence such as business justification. Although a prohibition as to sex discrimination is a dominant and recurring theme of international human rights law and utilized in many national contexts, such a prohibition lacks any single, unified form.

The analysis here begins by considering the application of sex discrimination protections in three key conventions – the *ICCPR*, the *ICESCR* and *CEDAW* – and its subsequent expansion in the jurisprudence of the treaty-bodies responsible for the implementation of those conventions – the Human Rights Committee (HRC), the Committee on Economic, Social and Cultural Rights (*CESCR*) and the *CEDAW* Committee and. It then considers how sex discrimination protection has been translated into domestic law in three countries – the United States, Australia, and India. Although there are multiple avenues

1 *Convention on the Elimination of All Forms of Discrimination against Women* 1979 (*CEDAW*) Article 1.

for sex discrimination claims in each country, the focus here is on the most utilized avenues in each of these jurisdictions. In the United States Title VII of the *Civil Rights Act* 1964 (Title VII) which prohibits sex discrimination in a range of employment practices is taken up, in Australia Section 5 of the *Sex Discrimination Act* 1984 (SDA) which prohibits sex discrimination in areas of public or quasi-public life, including employment, education, goods and services, accommodation, land and clubs is addressed,[2] and in India, Article 15(1) of the *Constitution of India* 1950 which prohibits any sex discrimination by the state is the focus. These three countries have been chosen for their legal similarities and their contextual differences. All three are common-law countries as colonized by Great Britain. They are all federations, democracies and have ratified or acceded to some or all of the international conventions that require states parties to prohibit sex discrimination. The United States and Australia however are perceived to fall into the category of 'western' legal cultures while India is seen as part of the 'Global South' with a hybrid legal system that is pluralistic, multilingual, and multiethnic.

This volume considers the expansion of the meaning of 'sex' to include in some jurisdictions, either through the jurisprudence of the courts or through legislation, characteristics that are so closely connected to sex that they have been held to constitute sex discrimination in themselves, for example, pregnancy, violence against women and sexual harassment. However, this volume does not consider case-law or developments when those aspects of 'sex' are protected in their own right. For example, if pregnancy is a specific protected ground in international human rights law or in domestic legislation, and case-law has developed around that specific ground, this volume does not consider those cases or developments.

This volume does, however, include gender as a protected ground of discrimination, and any related case-law. Sex and gender were differentiated as two discrete concepts in early feminist theoretical discussion.[3] Sex was categorized as referring to the biological differences between men and women. For example, the different reproductive systems of women and men were categorized as a difference based on sex.[4] Gender, by contrast was categorized as referring to the different socially constructed roles, behaviours, and attributes that a given society assigns to men and women, termed femininity and masculinity.[5] For example, women typically care for children because that is

2 *Sex Discrimination Act* 1984 (Cth), Part 2.

3 Judith Butler, 'Sex and Gender in Simone de Beauvoir's Second Sex' *Yale French Studies* 72 (1986), 35–49: 35.

4 *Ibid.*

5 Louise Chappell, 'Comparative Gender and Institutions Directions for Research Source' *Perspectives on Politics* 8(1) (2010), 183–189: 184.

the role assigned to them by society but because men can also provide care to children, although typically do not, this is classified as a gender, and not sex, difference.[6] Although the difference (or lack of difference) between sex and gender is extensively explored in feminist literature, both the international human rights framework and many domestic jurisdictions use the terms interchangeably. Some constitutions and anti-discrimination legislation include sex as a protected ground but not gender and some constitutions and anti-discrimination legislation include gender as a protected ground but not sex. Some (a few) include both.[7]

We consider both sex and gender in this volume as many claims of sex discrimination are grounded in normative gender rules and roles, rather than biological difference. For example, the women's movement in many countries first campaigned for women's right to vote, right to run for parliament, right to earn equal pay, and the right to work in the same professions as men.[8] The differentiation between men and women in these examples of inequality was based on the gender roles assigned to women and men and the stereotypes that have emerged through the application of those gender roles. For example, the view that women should focus on and prioritize domestic responsibilities led to the perception that she had no useful role in voting, that she was unsuitable for public office, and that men were financially responsible for the family and therefore should be paid higher wages.[9] Differentiation and discrimination based on sex as biological difference, rather than gender as socially constructed, is therefore much rarer. Indeed, the birthing process and related functions remain as the major source of biological sex difference and discrimination.[10]

This volume compares sex discrimination protection through three thematic lenses. Firstly, it charts and compares the evolution and development of sex discrimination protection in international human rights law in three

6 Hilary Lipps, *Sex and Gender: An Introduction* (Waveland Press, 2017).

7 *Constitution of the Republic of South Africa* 1996, Article 9(3) prohibits discrimination on the grounds of both sex and gender; *Constitution of India* 1950, s. 15(1) prohibits discrimination on the ground of sex but not gender; and *Constitution of the Democratic Republic of Timor Lester* 2010, Article 16(2) prohibits discrimination on the ground of gender but not sex.

8 Pamela Marie Paxton, Melanie M. Hughes, and Tiffany Barnes, *Women, Politics and Power: A Global Perspective*. (Rowman & Littlefield Publishers, 2020); Amrita Basu (ed.), *The Challenge of Local Feminisms: Women's Movements in Global Perspective* (Routledge, 2018).

9 Shan-Jan Sarah Liu, 'Cracking Gender Stereotypes? Challenges Women Political Leaders Face' *Political Insight* (2019), 12–15; Nicole Busby and Grace James, *A History of Regulating Working Families: Strains, Stereotypes, Strategies and Solutions* (Bloomsbury Publishing, 2020).

10 Anne-Marie Mooney Cotter, *Pregnant Pause: An International Legal Analysis of Maternity Discrimination* (Routledge, 2016).

treaty-bodies – the CEDAW Committee, the HRC and the CESCR. Secondly, it then takes up the evolution and development of sex discrimination protection in three domestic law frameworks – the United States, Australia and India. Finally, the development of sex discrimination protection in international law is compared with the development of sex discrimination protection in the domestic legal contexts of the three country examples, with the implications of that comparison analyzed. This volume seeks to show that despite differences in the way that international approaches to sex discrimination are translated into domestic law and differences in social, political and cultural contexts women face similar limitations in accessing justice through sex discrimination frameworks.

1.1 *Our Approach to Comparative Law*

Comparative law, in broad terms, is the study of differences and similarities between the legal systems and the laws of different countries. Different studies compare different aspects of legal systems and laws. For example, some studies identify, categorize and compare different legal systems, for example the common law, the civil law, socialist law, Canon law, Jewish Law, Islamic law, Hindu law, and Chinese law.[11] Other studies compare types of law, for example, constitutional law, or approaches to violence against women, or family law.[12] The aims of comparative law include attaining a deeper knowledge of different legal system or laws, exploring means of improving different legal systems or laws, comparing the ability of different solutions to solve similar problems in different legal systems, and providing insights into the (common) practice of transplanting law and legal institutions from one system to another.[13]

Consequently, there are several different approaches to a comparative law endeavor. The standard and 'classic' is the functional approach, which proposes that laws and legal system mechanisms that fulfil the same function in different countries or jurisdictions can be usefully compared.[14] The assumption underscoring the functional approach to comparative law is that the

11 Shkelzen Hasanaj, 'Europeanization through Migration Policies: Legislative Comparison between Civil Law Systems and Common Law Systems' *Academic Journal of Interdisciplinary Studies* 7(2) (2018), 73–77.

12 Michael Da Silva, 'International Constitutions and Comparative Constitutional Law' *Notre Dame Journal of International & Comparative Law* 10(2) (2020), 139–172: 143, 144; and Saptarshi Mandal and Sachin Dhawan, 'Religious Family Law and Legal Change in Comparative Perspective' *Jindal Global Law Review* 7(1) (2016), 1–8: 3.

13 Patrick Glenn, 'The Aims of Comparative Law' *Elgar Encyclopedia of Comparative Law* (Edward Elgar Publishing, 2nd ed., 2012).

14 Francesca Bignami (ed.), 'Introduction. A New Field: Comparative Law and Regulation' in *Comparative Law and Regulation* (Edward Elgar Publishing, 2016), 275–305.

legal systems of every society face the same problems, and although these problems may be solved by different means, the outcomes are often similar.[15] Functionalist comparative law compares legal systems in different ways. It can consider the various judicial responses to similar situations. It can compare institutions, both legal and non-legal, even doctrinally different ones, if they fulfil similar functions in different legal systems. A functionalist approach can also include 'better-law comparisons' – the 'better' of several laws is that which fulfils its function better than the others.[16] Functionalist comparative law is criticized, however, for its failure to consider and account for the different cultural, political, and social contexts of different regions and countries.[17] Critics claim that functionalism ignores difference and is insensitive to heterogeneity, ambiguities, and ambivalences.[18] It places western legal culture at the top of an implicit 'normative scale'[19] marking western legal culture as the starting point for comparative legal research and the yardstick to access, systemize, and evaluate non-western legal systems.[20]

Legal transplants, the 'moving of a rule or a system of law from one country to another, of from one people to another,' are also a subject of comparative law and common in the drafting or redrafting of constitutions.[21] Some argue that legal transplants are an impossibility for 'in order to translate a text without any change in meaning, one would have to transport its audience as well.'[22] These critics are not arguing replica provisions are not transferred, clearly they are, but that as soon as they are transferred their meaning and interpretation is shaped by the cultural, social and political context in which they now exist.

In our view comparative law provides an opportunity through which the reasoning of decision-makers can be evaluated and assessed to ensure it is rigorous and not shaped by subjective beliefs.[23] The right to be free from sex discrimination is a core right in human rights law. Sex discrimination occurs

15 Günter Frankenberg, 'Critical Comparisons: Re-thinking Comparative Law' *Harvard International Law Journal* 26 (1985), 411–456: 438.

16 Julie De Coninck, 'The Functional Method of Comparative Law: Quo Vadis?' *Rabels Zeitschrift für ausländisches und internationales Privatrecht/The Rabel Journal of Comparative and International Private Law* 2 (2010), 318–350: 324, 325.

17 Günter Frankenberg, *Comparative Law as Critique* (Edward Elgar Publishing, 2016).

18 De Coninck, above n. 16, at 324, 327.

19 De Coninck, above n. 16, at 328.

20 De Coninck, above n. 16, at 328.

21 John Gillespie, Pip Nicholson and Penelope Nicholson (eds.), *Law and Development and the Global Discourses of Legal Transfers* (Cambridge University Press, 2012).

22 Pierre Legrand, 'The Impossibility of 'Legal Transplants' *Maastricht Journal of European and Comparative Law* 4(2) (1997), 111–124.

23 Sandra Fredman, *Comparative Human Rights Law* (OUP, 2018), 4.

in every country and in every context and if outcomes differ it is important to understand whether this is because of important and relevant differences in context or whether it is a failure to implement a right. Posing the same questions might give different answers but those differences must be justified.[24] Sex discrimination differs in context, form, and prevalence in different countries and contexts. However, there are commonalities in those inequalities and therefore our starting point for comparing sex discrimination law is functionalist because we argue that women in all countries experience sex discrimination. For example, all women have a shared experience of violence directed at them because they are women although it takes different forms in different countries.[25] Dowry violence is prevalent in the subcontinent,[26] female genital cutting is prevalent in some African countries,[27] and domestic and family violence is prevalent in all western countries.[28] In all these examples of violence, women are overwhelmingly the victims and men are overwhelmingly the offenders.[29]

However, context is also important and a functional approach alone is insufficient to successfully compare approaches to sex discrimination across different countries and regions. In many instances, legal transplants have occurred when sex discrimination provisions have been directly drawn from another country's constitution or anti-discrimination legislation, rather than drawn from human rights conventions and modified to reflect the local context. Such legal transplants may have been orchestrated by a former colonizer and sometimes transferred by international drafters and 'rule of law' support organizations.[30] However, when examining the court's interpretation of those provisions, an understanding of the contexts of those different countries is essential to understanding the operation of sex discrimination law in that country. Our approach to comparing sex discrimination law seeks to identify similarities and differences in the way international law is translated into

24 *Ibid.*, at 5.

25 Karen Devries et al., 'The Global Prevalence of Intimate Partner Violence Against Women' *Science* 340(6140) (2013), 1527–1528.

26 Priya R. Banerjee, 'Dowry in 21st-Century India: The Sociocultural Face of Exploitation' *Trauma, Violence, and Abuse* 15(1) (2014), 34–40.

27 Heather Sipsma, Peggy G. Chen, Angela Ofori-Atta, Ukwuoma O. Ilozumba, Kapouné Karfo and Elizabeth H. Bradley, 'Female Genital Cutting: Current Practices and Beliefs in Western Africa' *Bulletin of the World Health Organization* 90 (2012), 120–127.

28 Samia Alhabib, Ula Nur and Roger Jones, 'Domestic Violence against Women: Systematic Review of Prevalence Studies' *Journal of Family Violence* 25(4) (2010), 369–382.

29 *Ibid.*

30 Jaakko Husa, 'Developing Legal System, Legal Transplants, and Path Dependence: Reflections on the Rule of Law' *The Chinese Journal of Comparative Law* 6(2) (2018), 129–150.

national constitutions and domestic anti-discrimination legislation and how it is interpreted in the courts in our three country examples. Our final analysis of those differences, however, will include, as much as is possible, consideration of the different contexts.[31]

1.2 *Organization of This Volume*

This volume comprises four parts: Part One being the introduction, identifies the scope and aims of the volume. This part delineates the functional approach to comparative law and situates our approach to comparative law. As this volume includes gender in its examination of sex as a protected ground, this part explains the rationale for that decision. Part Two sets out and maps the evolution of the ground of sex in international human rights law. It considers the form of sex discrimination protection in three human rights conventions – the *ICCPR*, the *ICESCR* and *CEDAW*. It explores the interpretation of that protection by the three treaty-bodies that monitor those conventions through their concluding observations, General Comments and General Recommendations and in complaints and inquiries heard in their capacity under Optional Protocols and other complaints processes. Part Three elucidates the translation of sex discrimination protection in international human rights law into the domestic law in three countries, the United States, Australia and India, focusing on the most utilized sex discrimination avenue in each.

Part Four provides a comparison between the three conventions and their interpretation by their respective treaty-bodies. It also gives a comparison between the three country examples, and a further comparison with the international law framework. It analyses the successes and limitations of international and domestic law to provide justice and equality to women concluding that the translation of sex discrimination protection from international human right conventions into domestic law has resulted in frameworks that are limited in their capacity to support the eradication of sex discrimination from women's lives.

Part 2: Sex as an Internationally-Protected Ground in Human Rights Law

This part analyses how sex as a protected ground of discrimination is approached, interpreted and applied in the international human rights framework established after the two world wars to restrain governments from

31 Jaye Ellis, 'General Principles and Comparative Law' *European Journal of International Law* 22(4) (2011), 949–971: 966.

human rights abuses and to map out commonly agreed standards of rights for all people.[32] The *Universal Declaration of Human Rights* 1945 was the first human rights instrument to include sex as a universally-protected ground of discrimination.[33] The next two key 'core' instruments outlining fundamental rights and freedoms of all persons are the *International Covenant on Civil and Political Rights* 1966 (ICCPR) and the *International Covenant on Economic, Social and Cultural Rights* 1966 (ICESCR) and both include sex as a protected ground.[34] They are followed by the *Convention on the Elimination of all Forms of Discrimination against Women* 1979 (CEDAW), which focuses specifically on sex discrimination and the rights of women.[35] The *Convention on the Rights of the Child* 1990 (CRC)[36] and the *Convention on the Protection of the Rights of All Migrant Workers and Members of Their Families* 1990 (IMWC) also include sex as a protected ground of discrimination.[37] The *Convention on the Rights of Persons with Disabilities* 2006 (CRPD) does not specifically include sex as a protected ground, however Article 4 requires states parties to recognize that women and girls with disabilities are subject to multiple discrimination.

This part traces the evolution of the interpretation of sex as a protected ground of discrimination in the *ICCPR*, the *ICESCR* and *CEDAW*, the three conventions that have the most expansive interpretations of sex discrimination developed by their respective monitoring bodies. This analysis examines each treaty-body's definition of the scope of sex as a protected ground. This scope includes, for example, whether characteristics intimately connected with sex, such as pregnancy, or gender such as sexual harassment are in place. Other aspects include whether discrimination is defined to include direct and indirect discrimination. The steps each treaty-body takes to determine

---

32 Sue Farran, *Human Rights in the South Pacific: Challenges and Changes* (Routledge Cavendish, 2009), 59; and Niamh Reilly, *Women's Human Rights. Seeking Gender Justice in a Globalizing Age* (Polity Press, 2010), 48.

33 *Universal Declaration of Human Rights* 1945. Article 1 states that '[a]ll human beings are born free and equal in dignity and rights.' Article 2 states that '[e]veryone is entitled to all the rights and freedoms set forth in the Universal Declaration without distinction of any kind, such as race, colour, sex, language, religion, political or other opinion, national or social origin, property, birth or other status.' Article 7 states that '[a]ll are equal before the law and are entitled without any discrimination to equal protection of the law.'

34 *International Covenant on Civil and Political Rights* (ICCPR) 1966, Article 2(1); and the *International Covenant on Economic, Social and Cultural Rights* (ICESCR) 1966, Article 2(2).

35 *Convention on the Elimination of all Forms of Discrimination against Women* (CEDAW) 1979, Article 1.

36 *Convention on the Rights of the Child* (CRC) 1990, Article 2(1).

37 *Convention on the Protection of the Rights of All Migrant Workers and Members of their Families* (IMWC) 1990, Article 1.

whether sex discrimination has occurred are also analysed, for example, who is a victim, requirements as to an opposite-sex comparator, an intent to discriminate on the ground of sex, and any defences such as justification if 'reasonable'. That analysis then forms the basis of comparison detailed in Part Four.

None of the conventions, including *CEDAW*, provide in their plain wording any detailed explanation of how and when sex discrimination in a given situation is to be identified by a judge, tribunal or other decision-maker. However, as seen below, the treaty-bodies that monitor each of these conventions (the HRC monitors *ICCPR*, the CESCR monitors the *ICESCR* and the *CEDAW* Committee monitors *CEDAW*) have provided more expansive definitions in their jurisprudence, consisting of the following. Firstly, the three treaty-bodies have issued authoritative statements or guidance to states parties on the meaning of substantive rights, the obligations of states parties, and other common issues in the form of either General Comments or General Recommendations.[38] Secondly, each treaty body, when it receives and examines periodic reports submitted by states parties on the implementation of their treaty obligations issues concluding observations which outline, often in considerable detail, the context of their obligations including in relation to sex discrimination.[39] Thirdly, the three treaty bodies receive and consider communications by individuals alleging violation of one or more of their human rights by a state party.[40] In resolving these communications, the treaty-bodies expand their jurisprudence on sex discrimination.[41] In addition, the *CEDAW* Committee and the HRC have a mechanism to conduct fact-finding inquiries which has also contributed to the development of the sex discrimination jurisprudence of the treaty-bodies.[42]

---

38 Dinah Shelton, 'The Legal Status of Normative Pronouncements of Human Rights Treaty Bodies' in Holger Hestermeyer, Doris Konig, Nele Matz-Luck, Volker Roben, Volker Seibert-Fohr, Peter Tobias Stall and Silja Voneky (eds.), *Coexistence, Cooperation and Solidarity* (Brill Nijhoff, 2012), 553–575: 556, 557; and Geir Ulfstein, 'Law-Making by Human Rights Treaty Bodies' in Rain Liivoja and Jarna Petman (eds.), *International Law-Making. Essays in Honour of Jan Klabbers* (Routledge, 2014), 249–257: 251.

39 Cecilia Medina, 'The Role of International Tribunals: Law-Making or Creative Interpretation' in *The Oxford Handbook of International Human Rights Law* (Cambridge University Press, 2013), 661.

40 Ilias Bantekas and Lutz Oette, *International Human Rights Law and Practice* (Cambridge University Press, 2013), 86.

41 Susanne Zwingel, 'A New Tool in the Toolbox: The Optional Protocol to the Convention' in *Translating International Women's Rights. The CEDAW Convention* (Palgrave MacMillan, 2016), 109–133.

42 Ekkehard Strauss, 'Monitoring and Fact Finding by UN Human Rights Mechanisms' in Monica Serrano and Thomas Weiss (eds.), *The International Politics of Human Rights* (Routledge, 2014), 93–112; and Northern Ireland and Alliance Choice, 'Submission of

The following sections overview the text of each convention and the jurisprudence of each treaty-body in relation to sex discrimination claims.

2.1 *International Covenant on Civil and Political Rights 1966*

The *ICCPR* provides limited guidance in its text as to sex discrimination. There are two entry points to a sex discrimination claim under the ICCPR. Firstly, Article 26 ICCPR provides stand-alone protection from sex discrimination. Article 26 ICCPR states that:

> All persons are equal before the law and are entitled without any discrimination to the equal protection of the law. In this respect, the law shall prohibit any discrimination and guarantee to all persons equal and effective protection against discrimination on any ground such as race, colour, sex, language, religion, political or other opinion, national or social origin, property, birth or other status.

Article 2(1) ICCPR provides a second entry point. Rather than prohibiting discrimination broadly, all rights are qualified by the requirement that they must be delivered without sex discrimination. States parties must 'respect and to ensure to all individuals the rights recognized in the present Convention, without distinction of any kind, such as race, colour, sex, language, religion, political or other opinion, national or social origin, property, birth or other statuses.'[43] The rights recognized in the *ICCPR*, which must therefore be guaranteed and enjoyed without sex discrimination, include physical integrity, in the form of the right to life and freedom from torture and slavery (Articles 6, 7, and 8); liberty and security of the person, in the form of freedom from arbitrary arrest and detention and the right to habeas corpus (Articles 9, 10, and 11); procedural fairness in law, in the form of rights to due process, a fair and impartial trial, the presumption of innocence, and recognition as a person before the law (Articles 14, 15, and 16); individual liberty, in the form of the freedoms of movement, thought, conscience and religion, speech, association and assembly, family rights, the right to a nationality, and the right to privacy (Articles 12, 13, 17–24); prohibition of any propaganda for war as well as any advocacy of national or religious hatred that constitutes incitement to discrimination, hostility or violence by law (Article 20); and political participation, including the right to the right to vote (Article 25).

Evidence to the *CEDAW* Committee Optional Protocol: Inquiry Procedure' *Transitional Justice Institute Research Paper* 15–01 (2015).

43 *ICCPR* 1966, Article 2(1).

The HRC is the body responsible for overseeing and advising states parties on the implementation of the *ICCPR*. It has developed an extensive jurisprudence on sex discrimination including two relevant General Comments and a significant body of case-law through its Views adopted in relation to individual complaints received under the communications process established by its Optional Protocol. General Comment No. 18 1989 on non-discrimination states that the term 'discrimination' in Article 2 *ICCPR* means any distinction, exclusion, restriction or preference which is based on sex and which has the purpose or effect of nullifying or impairing the recognition, enjoyment or exercise by all persons, on an equal footing, of all rights and freedoms.[44] This definition has several important components. Firstly, there must be a 'distinction, exclusion, restriction or preference' which is based on sex. That requirement has led to a further requirement to establish differentiation typically through the use of an opposite-sex comparator.[45] Secondly, the distinction, exclusion, restriction or preference must have the 'purpose or effect' of nullifying or impairing the recognition, enjoyment or exercise ..., on an equal footing, of all rights and freedoms. While purpose may require intent, the term effect means, conversely, that intent is unnecessary. Thirdly, the distinction, exclusion, restriction or preference which is based on sex must 'impair a woman's enjoyment of her rights'. General Comment No. 18 also states that while Article 2 limits the scope of the rights to be protected against discrimination to those provided for in the *ICCPR*, Article 26 does not specify such limitations. Instead, Article 26 provides a stand-alone autonomous right.[46] It prohibits discrimination in law or in any field regulated and protected by public authorities.[47] Article 26 therefore requires states parties to ensure there is no sex discrimination in legislation and in the implementation of legislation.[48] Finally, General Comment No. 18 states that 'not every differentiation of treatment will constitute discrimination, if the criteria for such differentiation are reasonable and objective and if the aim is to achieve a purpose which is legitimate under the Covenant.'[49] Thus, only if there is an illegitimate aim and an unreasonable relationship of

44 Human Rights Committee, *General Comment No. 18*, Non-Discrimination, 37th Session 1989, at para 7.

45 For example, see *Shirin Aumeeruddy-Cziffra and 19 Other Mauritian Women v. Mauritius*, CCPR/C/12/D/35/1978, UN Human Rights Committee (HRC) 9 April 1981.

46 General Comment No. 18, above n. 44, at para 12.

47 *Ibid.*

48 Daniel Moeckli, 'Equality and Non-Discrimination' in Stephanie Farrior (ed.), *Equality and Non-Discrimination in International Human Rights Law* (Taylor and Francis, 2015), 157–175: 162.

49 General Comment No. 18, above n. 44, at para 13.

proportionality between the differentiation and the reason for that differentiation is the differential treatment unjustified and constitutes discrimination.[50] Therefore, not all differentiation of treatment on the basis of sex is sex discrimination under the *ICCPR*.[51]

General Comment No. 28, issued a decade later in 2000, on Article 3 (Equality of Rights between Men and Women) explains that every right guaranteed in the *ICCPR* must be delivered without sex discrimination.[52] General Comment No. 28 also provides guidance, for the first time, on the identification of multiple discrimination, intersectionality, stating:

> Discrimination against women is often intertwined with discrimination on other grounds such as race, colour, language, religion, political or other opinion, national or social origin, property, birth or other status. States parties should address the ways in which any instances of discrimination on other grounds affect women in a particular way, and include information on the measures taken to counter these effects.[53]

Although the wording suggests a more complex and nuanced understanding of multiple discrimination is required, no guidance is provided as to how this might be achieved. General Comment No. 28 provides no further guidance, except through a range of examples of discrimination in women's lives, as to what the scope of sex discrimination is or how to determine whether sex discrimination has occurred.[54]

Indeed, it is the published Views of the HRC that provide the most detailed guidance on its evolving approach to sex discrimination and makes the most significant contribution to its jurisprudence. In the first case of sex discrimination published by the HRC in 1981, certain first tentative steps to formulating an approach to sex discrimination are evident. In the *Mauritian Women Case,*[55] twenty women argued that the immigration law of Mauritius, which granted automatic residence rights to a foreign woman who marries a Mauritian man

50 Bal Sokhi-Bulley, 'Non-Discrimination and Difference: The (Non-)Essence of Human Rights Law' (2010), 1–12: 3.

51 *Ibid.*

52 Human Rights Committee, *General Comment No. 28*, Article 3 (Equality of Rights between Men and Women) 68th Session 2000, at 4, 6.

53 *Ibid.*, at para 30.

54 Dianne Otto, 'Gender Comment: Why does the UN Committee on Economic, Social and Cultural Rights Need a General Comment on Women' *Canadian Journal of Women and the Law* 14 (2002), 1–53: 28.

55 *Shirin Aumeeruddy-Cziffra and 19 Other Mauritian Women v. Mauritius*, CCPR/C/12/D/35/1978, UN Human Rights Committee (HRC), 9 April 1981, at para 67.

but not to a foreign man who marries a Mauritian woman, was sex discrimination.[56] The authors argued a number of rights guaranteed in the ICCPR were violated in such a way that amounted to sex discrimination in accord with Article 2, but also in violation of the stand-alone right in Article 26.[57]

The first step in the communications process under the Optional Protocol is that the author must be a victim 'of a violation by that State Party of any of the rights set forth in the Covenant'.[58] The HRC determined that only the three women who were married to foreign men were victims.[59] It found breaches of Article 2(1) (which guarantees enjoyment of all protected rights without sex discrimination) in combination with Article 17(1) (arbitrary interference with family and home) and Article 23(1) (protection of the family) and Article 26 (the stand alone provision which guarantees a right to be free from sex discrimination).[60] Although the case represents a straightforward example of direct discrimination, the reasoning that underscores the positive sex discrimination outcome is significant. The HRC made two comparisons. Firstly, it compared women with men, similarly situated – the three women married to non-national men were compared to national men married to non-national women – and found differentiation.[61] In a second comparison they compared women with similarly-situated women – the three women married to non-national men were compared to national women married to national men – and again found differentiation.[62] It found that both comparisons resulted in the women being disadvantaged because they were women. Focusing primarily on the first comparison (the three national women married to non-national men compared to national men married to non-national women), the HRC found that by creating a precarious residence status for their husbands, the family life of the three women was negatively affected.[63] By comparison. the non-national wives whose lives were not made precarious by the law, did not experience a similar negative effect in their family life.[64]

Having found differentiation on the basis of sex through both Article 2(1) and Article 26 ICCPR, the HRC stated 'no sufficient justification for this

56 *Ibid.*, at para 1.

57 The authors argued violations of Article 2, Article 3, Article 4, Article 17, Article 23, Article 25 and Article 26, *ibid.*, at para 5.1.

58 *Optional Protocol to the International Covenant on Civil and Political Rights* 1976, Article 1.

59 *Shirin Aumeeruddy-Cziffra*, above n. 55, at para 9.2(a).

60 *Ibid.*, at para 9.2(b)(i); and 9.2(b)2(ii).

61 *Ibid.*, at para 9.2(b)2(i)6.

62 *Ibid.*, at para 9.2(b)2(i)6.

63 *Ibid.*

64 *Ibid.*

difference has been given'[65] signaling that where there is a sufficient justification (in accord with General Comment No. 18) then sex discrimination will not be found. There was no discussion, or suggestion, that an intent to discriminate was necessary. Any consideration of multiple discrimination by the HRC was dismissed by its proclamation that: 'a differentiation which appears on one level to be one of [marital] status is in fact one of sex, placing married women at a disadvantage compared with married men.'[66] Arguably, however, the women were discriminated against, in comparison to the wives of Mauritius nationals, by both their sex and their marital status. As will be seen in subsequent cases the HRC does not effectively develop interpretations of multiple discriminations.[67]

A decade later, the HRC published its 1988 Views in *Graciela Ato del Avellanal v. Peru.*[68] In this case, a Peruvian woman who owned two apartment buildings in Lima was prevented from suing the tenants to collect overdue rents because, under Article 168 of the Peruvian *Civil Code* 1852, when a woman is married, only her husband is entitled to pursue an action in relation to property of the marriage before the courts. Avellanal argued Article 168 was sex discrimination because the discrimination she faced was only because she was a woman.[69] The HRC agreed, without making any express comparison to similarly-situated men or assessing justifiability and stated Article 26 *ICCPR* was violated.[70] Since the discrimination was direct, and Avellanal was clearly discriminated against on the basis of sex in comparison to her husband, the HRC may have seen no need to explicitly compare the situation of the author with similarly-situated men. The HRC ordered Peru to 'take effective measures to remedy the violations suffered by the victim.'[71]

In 1992 the HRC published its Views in *Nicholas Toonen v. Australia.*[72] Toonen argued that two provisions of the Tasmanian *Criminal Code* 1924,

65 *Ibid.*, at para 9.2(b)(2)(i)8.

66 Hugo Storey, 'The Right to Family Life and Immigration Case Law, at Strasbourg' *International and Comparative Law Quarterly* 39(2) (1990), 328–344; and Rebecca Cook, 'International Human Rights Law Concerning Women: Case Notes and Comments' *Vanderbilt Journal of Transnational Law* 23 (1990), 779–818.

67 Shreya Atrey, 'Fifty Years On: The Curious Case of Intersectional Discrimination in the ICCPR' *Nordic Journal of Human Rights* 35(3) (2017), 220–239: 227, 228.

68 *Graciela Ato del Avellanal v. Peru*, Communication No. 202/1986, U.N. Doc. Supp. No. 40 (A/44/40) UN Human Rights Committee (1988).

69 *Ibid.*, at para 2.1.

70 *Ibid.*, at para 10.2.

71 *Ibid.*, at para 12.

72 *Toonen v. Australia*, Communication No. 488/1992, U.N. Doc CCPR/C/50/D/488/1992 UN Human Rights Committee (1994).

which criminalized various forms of consenting sexual contact between men in private, violated Article 2(1) *ICCPR* coupled with Article 17 (right to privacy) and also Article 26, constituting sex discrimination.[73] Sexual orientation is not a protected ground in the *ICCPR*. Australia agreed that it was a distinction on the ground of sex, but only because the legislation criminalized men and not women, and sought the guidance of the HRC as to whether sexual orientation could be included through the term '... or other status' in Article 26 *ICCPR*.[74] The HRC stated that in its view, there was no need to draw on the 'any other status' provision because the term 'sex' in Articles 2(1) and 26 ICCPR include sexual orientation.[75]

In 1999 the HRC published its Views in *Hendrica Vos v. The Netherlands*[76] a more nuanced case than many of the cases of direct discrimination that preceded it. Vos was receiving a disability allowance under the *General Disablement Benefits Act* (AAW) but when her ex-husband died, her allowance ceased as she became eligible for a different allowance established by the *General Widows and Orphans Act* (AWW).[77] Under the latter, she received less than she had been receiving under the former. Vos argued that forcing her to shift allowances, and the subsequent loss of income, constituted sex discrimination.[78] The HRC held, firstly, that although the right to social security was not protected by the *ICCPR* (the *ICESCR* which did not have a complaints process), it could still be a breach of Article 2 *ICCPR* (guarantee of all the rights in the convention free from sex discrimination) because protection from sex discrimination extended beyond the rights protected by the *ICCPR*[79] as well as Article 26 *ICCPR* (stand-alone protection from sex discrimination). However, the HRC found there was no sex discrimination because, although they agreed that the AAW operated to make the author worse-off financially, the rationale underlying the legislation is to benefit women as after a married man dies his widow may have insufficient means of subsistence, and therefore it was not sex discrimination.[80]

The weaknesses of the decision are multiple. Firstly, if a woman is worse-off financially because of a law or policy, because she is a woman (as in this case),

73 *Ibid.*, at para 3.1.
74 *Ibid.*, at para 6.9.
75 *Ibid.*, at para 8.7.
76 *Hendrika S. Vos v. The Netherlands*, Communication No. 218/1986, U.N. Doc. CCPR/C/35/D/218/1986) UN Human Rights Committee (1989).
77 *Ibid.*, at para 2.1.
78 *Ibid.*, at para 10.1.
79 *Ibid.*, at para 11.2.
80 *Ibid.*, at para 12.

surely the fact that no man could be in this position constitutes a differentiation on the basis of sex. Additionally, in contrast, the HRC in the *Mauritian Women Case* made a comparison between the three women married to non-nationals and (differently placed) women who were married to national men. A similar comparison in Vos between the author's position and disabled women who are not widows would have led to a finding of a differentiation. Secondly, the HRC placed weight on the fact that the intent of the legislation was not discriminatory (indeed the opposite) to conclude it was not sex discrimination.[81] Yet General Comment No. 18 clearly states that while sex discrimination can result if the purpose is discriminatory, it can also result if the effect is discriminatory. In this case, the effect was surely discriminatory since no disabled widower could be in the disadvantaged position that Vos found herself. Finally, Vos is not arguing that the benefit the legislation intends to bestow is inherently discriminatory, rather it is the rule that extinguishes eligibility to the AWA, regardless of whether it places a person in a worse financial situation, that is discriminatory. The HRC focused on the legislation and its overall beneficial intent rather than the rule of eligibility, which is curious, since the rule could be easily modified to ensure that no individual sex discrimination occurs without detracting from the overall benefit which the legislation intends, and in fact provides, to many widows.[82]

In 2011 the HRC published its Views in *L.N.P. v. Argentina*,[83] a more nuanced case than many of the previous cases because of the multiple discriminations at play.[84] A 15-year-old girl, P from a marginalized ethnic minority group – Qom – in Argentina, was sexually assaulted by three men. She immediately reported the attack to the police, however she was kept waiting for hours at the police station, then subsequently at a medical centre where eventually anal and vaginal examinations were performed. A social worker was sent to interview P's neighbours and relatives about her sexual history and morals as part of the investigation. The three accused were ultimately acquitted following a trial solely in Spanish, despite this not being the first language of P and several of the key witnesses. Significant reliance was placed on P's sexual history by the prosecution and the judge.[85] P argued a violation of Article 2(1) ICCPR coupled with Article 7 (right to be free from torture), Article 14 (access

81 *Ibid.*

82 Tufyal Choudhury, 'The Human Rights Committee's Interpretation of ICCPR Article 26' *European Human Rights Law Review* 1 (2003), 24–52.

83 *L.N.P. v. Argentine Republic*, Communication No. 1610/2007, U.N. Doc. CCPR/C/102/D/1610/2007) UN Human Rights Committee (2011).

84 Shreya Atrey, *Intersectional Discrimination* (Oxford University Press, 2019), 17–19, 135–136.

85 *L.N.P. v. Argentine Republic*, above n. 83, at para 3.2.

to justice), Article 17 (right to be free from arbitrary interference with privacy, family and home) and Article 24 (right to protection as a minor free from sex discrimination).[86] She also argued sex discrimination under the stand-alone sex discrimination protection of Article 26.[87] The HRC concluded that the facts did reveal the existence of discrimination based on the author's sex in violation of Article 26.[88] In relation to the other rights, the HRC did not focus directly on sex discrimination, finding that her rights were violated under these Articles on their own terms.[89] The HRC took no account of the multiple discriminations at play (despite the direction in General Comment No. 18 to do so) and did not comment on or challenge the gender, youth and racial stereotypes deployed in the case – for example that as a young woman from a marginalized ethnic minority group, she was sexually promiscuous.[90] Remedies and sanctions were also weak. The HRC requested full implementation of the compensatory measures previously agreed upon (but not paid) between the author and Argentina through the amicable settlement procedure. The HRC also recommended that Argentina ensure that similar violations are not perpetrated in the future, in particular by guaranteeing access for victims of sexual assault to the courts in conditions of equality.[91]

In 2015 the HRC published its Views in *M.T. v. Uzbekistan*.[92] M.T., an Uzbekistan national, was first arrested in 2002 by two police officers, and interrogated about her human rights activities, beaten and threatened with rape. In 2005 she was arrested again and interrogated about her human rights activities and accused of spreading propaganda against the Uzbekistan government. Subsequently, a police officer took her to an office where three unidentified men beat her and took turns in raping her several times until she lost consciousness. She was eventually released the same day without charge. Six months later thirty heavily-armed police officers arrested her and charged her with extortion. She was convicted and imprisoned. She was forced to work nine hours a day, physically attacked by prison wardens, forced to stand naked in the cold until she lost consciousness resulting in a deterioration of her health and was involuntarily sterilized. M.T. argued (amongst other things) that the

86 *Ibid.*, at para 3.1.
87 *Ibid.*, at para 3.1.
88 *Ibid.*, at para 13.3.
89 *Ibid.*, at para 13.4–13.9.
90 Shreya Atrey, 'Fifty Years On: The Curious Case of Intersectional Discrimination in the ICCPR' *Nordic Journal of Human Rights* 35(3) (2017), 220–239: 229.
91 *L.N.P. v. Argentine Republic*, above n. 83, at para 14.
92 *M.T. v.* Uzbekistan, Communication No. 2234/2013 U.N. Doc CCPR/C/114/D/2234/2013, UN Human Rights Committee, 21 October 2015.

gang rape and the involuntary sterilization constituted sex discrimination under Article 26 ICCPR.[93] The HRC agreed, stating that sexual abuse is a form of extreme gender-based violence,[94] and that both the rapes and the sterilization represented specific aggressions against her as a woman.[95] According to the majority, once gender-based violence is established, no further steps are necessary to satisfy the stand-alone sex discrimination protection of Article 26.[96] The HRC recommended carrying out an impartial, effective and thorough investigation into the allegations of torture and ill-treatment, initiating criminal proceedings against those responsible, providing the author with appropriate compensation and taking steps to prevent similar violations occurring in the future.[97]

In a dissent, committee member Dheerujlall Seetulsingh stated that although *M.T.* was the victim of severe violence of a sexual nature, it was not sex discrimination. The involuntary sterilization also was not sex discrimination.[98] Seetulsingh reasoned, utilizing an opposite-sex comparator approach, that men could be victims of sexual violence and subjected to cruel punishment. In another comparison, Seetulsingh reasoned that there was no evidence other women in similar circumstances are subjected to such horrible treatment. She stated: 'The fact that one individual undergoes such treatment by force is no pointer towards discrimination as such under Article 26.'[99] Although a dissenting opinion, the view that sexual violence is not gendered because men can be victims weakens the important step taken by the HRC to identify violence against women as sex discrimination.

Two recent cases on abortion laws in Ireland have further tested (and expanded) the HRC's reasoning on sex discrimination. The HRC published its Views in *Mellet v. Ireland* in 2016 and *Siobhán Whelan v. Ireland* in 2017.[100] Mellet became pregnant in 2011, and in her twenty-first week of pregnancy, she found out that the foetus had congenital heart defects. She was told by her medical practitioner that, even if the impairment meant the foetus could not live, she could not have a termination of her pregnancy in Ireland. The

93 *Ibid.*, at para 3.10.
94 *Ibid.*, at para 7.4.
95 *Ibid.*, at para 7.6.
96 *Ibid.*, at para 7.6.
97 *Ibid.*, at para 7.6.
98 *Ibid.* Appendix 1, at para 5.
99 *Ibid.* Appendix 1, at para 5.
100 *Mellet v. Ireland* Communication. No. 2324/2013, UN Doc. CCPR/C/116/D/2324/2013 UN Human Rights Committee (2016); and *Siobhán Whelan v. Ireland* Communication No. 2425/2014, UN Doc CCPR/C/119/D/2425/2014 (2017).

medical practitioner told her 'some people in your situation may choose to travel' but gave her no further information about her options.[101] In the second case, Whelan's obstetrician similarly in the twentieth week of her second pregnancy diagnosed the foetus with holoprosencephaly, a congenital brain malformation with a three percent survival rate to delivery. The obstetrician stated that 'in another jurisdiction [they] would be offered a termination but obviously not in this country due to Irish law.'[102] Whelan, like Mellet, was not given further information and was not referred to anyone to discuss the diagnosis, the care she would be offered in Ireland or the possibility of travelling abroad to terminate the pregnancy. Instead, the obstetrician stated that she 'would continue with the pregnancy, attend ante-natal appointments "as normal" and wait for nature to take its course.'[103]

The authors in both cases argued that Ireland's abortion law criminalizing abortion violated several protected rights in the *ICCPR* as it constituted sex and gender discrimination. They argued breaches of Article 7 (cruel, inhuman and degrading treatment), Article 17 (right to privacy) and Article 19 (right to freedom of information) in their own right, and additionally that they experienced sex discrimination in relation to each of these rights in violation of Article 2(1).[104] They also argued sex discrimination under Article 26 on the basis that the laws resulted in the health services failing to accommodate the fundamental biological differences between men and women in reproduction.[105] The authors utilized a broad opposite-sex comparator approach to argue there are no similar restrictions on health services that only men need. Indeed, the Irish abortion ban traumatizes and 'punishes' women who are in need of terminating their non-viable pregnancies while male patients in Ireland are not subjected to such treatment when seeking any necessary medical care.[106] In countering the arguments of the authors in relation to Article 26, Ireland drew upon a classic narrow comparison between similarly-situated men and women to argue that its abortion law did not constitute sex discrimination because there are no similarly-situated men with whom to compare the authors.[107]

101 *Mellet v. Ireland*, above n. 100, at para 2.1.

102 *Siobhán Whelan v. Ireland*, above n. 100, at para 2.1.

103 *Ibid.*, at para 2.1.

104 *Ibid.*, at para 3.1–3.8; and *Mellet v. Ireland*, above n. 100, at para 3.1–3.14.

105 *Siobhán Whelan v. Ireland*, above n. 100, at para 3.9–3.11; and *Mellet v. Ireland*, above n. 100, at para 3.15–3.20.

106 *Siobhán Whelan v. Ireland*, above n. 100, at para 3.9; and *Mellet v. Ireland*, above n. 100, at para 3.16.

107 *Siobhán Whelan v. Ireland*, above n. 100, at para 4.13; and *Mellet v. Ireland*, above n. 100, at para 4.13.

They argued there is no 'invidious discrimination' as their physical circumstances during pregnancy are inherently different and cannot be compared to men.[108] If there was a valid differentiation (that pregnant women could be compared to non-pregnant men), Ireland argued in the alternative it should be considered 'a reasonable and objective differentiation' within its 'margin of appreciation' because the criminalization of abortion was in pursuit of the legitimate aim of protecting the foetus and the law is proportionate to that aim striking a fair balance between the rights of the foetus which is capable of being born alive, the community and the rights of a pregnant woman.[109] The law offered a 'nuanced and proportionate response to the views of the Irish electorate on the highly politicised and divisive question of the extent to which the right to life of the foetus should be balanced against the rights of the woman.'[110]

In the end, the HRC did not consider sex discrimination in relation to Articles 7, 17 and 24 ICCPR which it found were violated in their own right.[111] The HRC, however, did find a breach of Article 26 in both cases, and sex discrimination as a result. The HRC made no comparison of women with men but instead compared women pregnant with a foetus with a fatal impairment who nevertheless decided to carry the foetus to term with hypothetical pregnant women who chose to travel to terminate the pregnancy in another country.[112] This is similar to how the HRC approached the authors in the *Mauritius Women Case* where they also compared women with differently-situated women. The HRC found differentiation because women continuing with the pregnancy would receive the full protection of the public health-care system. By contrast, women who chose to terminate a non-viable pregnancy must rely on their own financial resources to do so, entirely unsupported by the public

108 *Siobhán Whelan v. Ireland*, above n. 100, at para 4.13; and *Mellet v. Ireland*, above n. 100, at para 4.13.

109 *Siobhán Whelan v. Ireland*, above n. 100, at para 4.14; and *Mellet v. Ireland*, above n. 100, at para 4.14.

110 *Siobhán Whelan v. Ireland*, above n. 100, at para 7.4–7.9; and *Mellet v. Ireland*, above n. 100, at para 4.14.

111 *Siobhán Whelan v. Ireland*, above n. 100, at para 7.4–7.9; and *Mellet v. Ireland*, above n. 100, at para 7.4–7.8.

112 *Siobhán Whelan v. Ireland*, above n. 100, at para 7.12; and *Mellet v. Ireland*, above n. 100, at para 7.11. See for more extensive discussion Katarzyna Sękowska-Kozłowska, 'A Tough Job: Recognizing Access to Abortion as a Matter of Equality. A Commentary on the Views of the UN Human Rights Committee in the Cases of *Mellet v. Ireland* and *Whelan v. Ireland*' *Reproductive Health Matters* 26(54) (2018), 25–31.

health-care system.[113] After these two cases, and in combination with internal and external pressures, Ireland conducted a referendum in 2018 to replace the Eighth Amendment, which gives the life of the foetus the same value as that of its mother, with a clause permitting the Oireachtas (parliament) to legislate for the termination of pregnancies. The referendum was overwhelmingly in favor of the amendment. The Irish Constitution was amended, and the Health (Regulation of Termination of Pregnancy) Act 2018 was enacted, making abortion lawful during the first twelve weeks of pregnancy, and after 12 weeks in cases where the pregnant woman's life or health is at risk, or in the case of a fatal foetal abnormality.[114]

In 2019 the HRC published its findings in Sharon McIvor and Jacob Grismer v. Canada,[115] its most recent sex discrimination case. The HRC found that First Nations women in Canada and their descendants had been discriminated against on the ground of sex in violation of Article 26 because of status requirements under the *Indian Act 1876*.[116] The authors were descendants of Mary Tom, a First Nations woman and member of the Lower Nicola Band born in 1888. Susan was born in 1925 to Mary Tom and a Dutch father. The *Indian Act*, at the time, denied Susan's registration as a First Nations person, because it transmitted First Nations status through the male line, and not through matrilineal descent. Susan's daughter Sharon, the first author, was also unable to be registered as a First Nations person. She married a non-First Nation person and her son Jacob, the second author, was also denied status as a First Nations person.[117] Although new legislation gave men and women equal ability to confer First Nations status, it was not retrospective for some First Nations women, including Sharon. In contrast, Sharon's brother was able to transmit full status to his descendants.[118]

The authors argued that lack of status meant an inability to access extended health benefits and post-secondary education funding for their children as provided for First Nations children.[119] Canada accepted this as sex discrimination given the straightforward comparison with Sharon's brother whose children

113 *Siobhán Whelan v. Ireland*, above n. 100, at para 7.12; and *Mellet v. Ireland*, above n. 100, at para 7.11.

114 Anna Carnegie and Rachel Roth, 'From the Grassroots to the Oireachtas: Abortion Law Reform in the Republic of Ireland' *Health and Human Rights* 21(2) (2019), 109–120.

115 *Sharon McIvor and Jacob Grismer v. Canada* Communication No. 2020/2010, UN Doc. CCPR/C/124/D/2020/2010 UN Human Rights Committee (2019).

116 *Ibid.*, at para 7.11.

117 *Ibid.*, at para 2.3, 2.7.

118 *Ibid.*, at para 2.6, 2.7, 2.8.

119 *Ibid.*, at para 3.2.

were able to access these benefits.[120] The authors also argued the consequences of the lack of status and ability to transmit status included being regarded as 'inferior and less Indian'.[121] Canada argued that such discrimination was perpetrated by the community and not the law.[122] The HRC found however that the prohibition on sex discrimination in the *ICCPR* applies not only to discrimination in law, but also to discrimination in fact, whether practised by public authorities, by the community, or by private persons or bodies.[123]

Finally, Canada argued that the differentiation 'is justified by the legitimate aim of preservation of acquired rights'.[124] However, the HRC found that Canada had not demonstrated how recognizing equal status for Sharon and Jacob would adversely affect the acquired rights of others.[125] The HRC concluded that Canada failed to demonstrate that the stated-aim was based on objective and reasonable grounds and recommended Canada take steps to address residual discrimination within First Nations communities arising from the legal discrimination based on sex in the *Indian Act*.[126]

2.2 *International Covenant on Economic, Social and Cultural Rights 1966*

The *ICESCR*, like the *ICCPR* provides limited guidance in its text regarding sex discrimination. Article 2(1) ICESCR requires states parties 'to respect and to ensure to all individuals the rights recognized in the present Convention, without distinction of any kind, such as race, colour, sex, language, religion, political or other opinion, national or social origin, property, birth or other statuses.'

The rights protected by *ICESCR* include rights to work, under 'just and favourable conditions' including the right to form and join trade unions (Articles 6, 7, and 8); the right to social security, including social insurance (Article 9); the right to family life, including paid parental leave and the protection of children (Article 10); the right to an adequate standard of living, including adequate food, clothing and housing, and the 'continuous improvement of living conditions' (Article 11); the right to health, specifically 'the highest attainable

120 *Ibid.*, at para 5.6.
121 *Ibid.*, at para 3.2.
122 *Ibid.*, at para 5.31.
123 *Ibid.*, at para 7.11.
124 *Ibid.*, at para 5.12.
125 *Ibid.*, at para 7.11.
126 *Ibid.*, at para 9. See Shelagh Day, 'Equal Status for Indigenous Women-Sometime, Not Now: The Indian Act and Bill S-3' *Canadian Woman Studies* 33(1/2) (2018), 174–185; and Gwen Brodsky, 'Indian Act Sex Discrimination: Enough Inquiry Already, Just Fix It' *Canadian Journal of Women and the Law* 28(2) (2016), 314–320.

standard of physical and mental health' (Article 12); and the right to education, including free universal primary education, generally available secondary education and equally accessible higher education. These should be directed to 'the full development of the human personality and the sense of its dignity' and enable all persons to participate effectively in society (Articles 13 and 14) and finally participation in cultural life (Article 15).

All of these rights, in accord with Article 2(1), must be recognized without sex discrimination. Unlike the *ICCPR,* the *ICESCR* does not have a stand-alone article that prohibits sex-discrimination in its own right, as equality and non-discrimination is considered a civil right rather than a social right. Sex discrimination therefore must be established in relation to the rights protected by the *ICESCR*.

The Committee on Economic, Social and Cultural Rights (*CESCR*) is a body of eighteen independent experts that monitors implementation of the *ICESCR* by its states parties. Its jurisprudence on sex discrimination is largely constructed through its concluding observations and through General Comments Nos. 16 and 20.[127] The Optional Protocol to the *ICESCR* only entered into force in May 2013. The Protocol provides the CESCR with the competence to receive and consider communications from individuals claiming that their rights under the *ICESCR* have been violated, including on the ground of sex discrimination. There are only five published Views, of which only one is a sex discrimination complaint.[128] The *CESCR* may also, under certain circumstances, undertake inquiries on grave or systematic violations of any of the economic, social and cultural rights in the *ICESCR* and consider inter-state complaints, however to date none have been undertaken.[129]

The *CESCR* issued General Comment No. 16 to expand and explain the meaning of sex discrimination in relation to economic, social and cultural rights.[130] Importantly, the comment states that 'discrimination must be eliminated both formally and substantively' and that both direct and indirect forms of differential treatment can amount to discrimination.[131] Direct discrimination 'occurs

127 Committee on Economic, Social and Cultural Rights, *General Comment No. 16, The Equal Right of Men and Women to the Enjoyment of All Economic, Social and Cultural Rights (Art. 3 of the Covenant)* 34th Session 2005.

128 *Marcia Cecilia Trujillo Calero v. Ecuador* Communication. No. 10/2015, UN Doc. E/C.12/63/D/10/2015 UN Human Rights Committee (2018).

129 General Assembly, *Optional Protocol to the International Covenant on Economic, Social and Cultural Rights* 10 December 2008 (A/RES/63/117), Article 10 and Article 11.

130 Meghan Campbell, 'Monitoring Women's Socio-Economic Equality under the ICESCR.' *Canadian Journal of Women and the Law* 30(1) (2018), 82–116: 87.

131 *General Comment No. 16*, above n. 127, at para 13.

when an individual is treated less favourably than another person in a similar situation for a reason related to a prohibited ground'.[132] Indirect discrimination refers to 'laws, policies or practices which appear neutral at face value, but have a disproportionate impact on the exercise of Covenant rights as distinguished by prohibited grounds of discrimination.'[133] For instance, requiring that all employees work full-time may indirectly discriminate against women who often have domestic responsibilities preventing them from full-time employment. Finally, General Comment No. 16 states that: 'Gender-based violence is a form of discrimination that inhibits the ability to enjoy rights and freedoms, including economic, social and cultural rights, on a basis of equality.'[134]

General Comment No. 20 was issued in 2009 and further clarifies the CESCR approach to sex discrimination.[135] It states that sex discrimination must be eliminated 'both formally and substantively'.[136] This requires not 'merely comparing the formal treatment of individuals in similar situations'.[137] Indeed, direct discrimination 'includes detrimental acts or omissions on the basis of prohibited grounds where there is no comparable similar situation' (for example, pregnancy).[138] This requires states parties to adopt measures 'to ensure individuals and entities in the private sphere do not discriminate on prohibited grounds.'[139] Multiple discriminations when individuals or groups of individuals face discrimination on more than one prohibited ground 'merits particular consideration and remedying'.[140]

In 2018 the CESCR published its only decision to date on sex discrimination (*Marcia Cecilia Trujillo Calero v. Ecuador*).[141] The author argued that her right to social security (Article 9 ICESCR) was violated on the ground of sex (Article 2(2)) when she was denied a retirement pension. To be eligible for the retirement pension 300 consecutive contributions were required. Calero had failed to make contributions for six consecutive months, and although she resumed her contributions and had in total made over 300 contributions

---

132 *Ibid.*, at para 12.
133 *Ibid.*, at para 13.
134 *Ibid.*, at para 27.
135 Committee on Economic, Social and Cultural Rights *General Comment No. 20, Non-discrimination in Economic, Social and Cultural Rights (Art. 2, para. 2, of the Covenant)* 42nd Session 2 July 2009.
136 *Ibid.*, at para 8.
137 *Ibid.*, at para 8.
138 *Ibid.*, at para 10(a).
139 *Ibid.*, at para 11.
140 *Ibid.*, at para 17.
141 *Calero*, above n. 128.

she was not entitled to a retirement pension.[142] Calero argued she was part of a generation of women who dedicated the majority of their lives to unpaid domestic work, and that she faced greater obstacles than men in making uninterrupted contributions.[143] Indeed, under the scheme unpaid female domestic workers had to contribute on the same basis as independent workers, including professionals, despite not having a salary, in order to meet entitlement under the legislation thus placing them at a disadvantage compared to independent workers, most of whom had fixed incomes.[144] This is an important case as it involved both indirect discrimination and multiple discriminations on the basis of both gender and age. Ecuador argued that the requirement for 300 consecutive contributions is gender neutral and therefore does not constitute sex discrimination.[145]

The CESCR found that Article 2 ICESCR, viewed alongside the right to social security guaranteed in Article 9, meant that social security schemes must not discriminate against women in law or in fact.[146] In particular, social security schemes must eschew persistent stereotypes and other structural causes which result in women's exclusion particularly if they are engaged disproportionately in unpaid work or part-time work.[147] Ecuador, because it did not take steps to eliminate the factors that prevent women from making equal contributions to social security schemes, violated Article 9 on the ground of sex. The CESCR further noted that the intersection of both gender and age discrimination made the author particularly vulnerable to discrimination in comparison with the general population.[148] The CESCR recommended that Ecuador compensate the victim and take steps to ensure the social security scheme does not discriminate indirectly against women in the future.[149]

2.3 *Convention on the Elimination of All Forms of Discrimination against Women 1979*

CEDAW provides in its text much more guidance on the identification of sex discrimination than either the ICESCR or the ICCPR. CEDAW has been described as utilizing 'general and far-reaching language' which has enabled the CEDAW Committee 'to be creative and progressive in their interpretation

142 *Ibid.*, at para 3.2.
143 *Ibid.*, at para 3.4.
144 *Ibid.*, at para 3.5.
145 *Ibid.*, at para 4.10.
146 *Ibid.*, at para 13.4.
147 *Ibid.*, at para 13.4.
148 *Ibid.*, at para 19.2.
149 *Ibid.*, at para 22–24.

and application of the Convention'.[150] Indeed, Article 1 CEDAW provides a comprehensive definition of sex discrimination to include:

> [A]ny distinction, exclusion or restriction made on the basis of sex which has the effect or purpose of impairing or nullifying the recognition, enjoyment or exercise by women, irrespective of their marital status, on a basis of equality of men and women, of human rights and fundamental freedoms in the political, economic, social, cultural, civil or any other field.

Article 2 establishes the framework for the subsequent substantive Articles 6–16 and is central to the obligations of states parties under CEDAW.[151] It requires states parties to condemn sex discrimination in all its forms, covering all discrimination even if not specifically identified in CEDAW. States parties are to pursue by all appropriate means, and without delay (no justification for delay is permissible including lack of financial and technical resources) a policy of eliminating discrimination against women. Uniquely, while other international human rights conventions (such as the ICCPR and the ICESCR) are limited to the conduct of states parties and their representatives, Article 2 also requires states parties to eliminate sex discrimination against women by any person, organization or enterprise. The extension of anti-discrimination protection beyond state actors to include non-state actors is indicative of the recognition that to effectively combat sex discrimination in all areas of women's lives, the regulation of both state and non-state actors throughout the public and private spheres of women's lives is required.

Articles 6–16 identify particular areas of women's lives in which sex discrimination must therefore be prohibited. These areas include all forms of traffic in women and exploitation of the prostitution of women (Article 6); political representation and participation (Article 7); opportunities to represent governments at the international level (Article 8); acquiring, changing or retaining nationality and to pass on their nationality to their children (Article 9); the field of education (Article 10); the field of employment (Article 11); the field of health care (Article 12); the right to family benefits and to bank loans, mortgages and other forms of financial credit (Article 13); discrimination against

150 Jim Murdoch, 'Unfulfilled Expectations: The Optional Protocol to the Convention on the Elimination of All Forms of Discrimination against Women' *European Human Rights Law Review* 1 (2010), 26–46: 33.

151 CEDAW Committee, General Recommendation 28, *Core Obligations of States under Article 2 of the Convention on the Elimination of All Forms of Discrimination against Women* 47th Session 16 December 2010.

rural women (Article 14); equality with men before the law and civil matters (Article 15); and finally marriage and family relations (Article 16).

The definition of discrimination in Article 1 *CEDAW* is important because it provides guidance in recognizing and identifying sex discrimination.[152] Firstly, Article 1 refers to any distinction, exclusion or restriction made on the basis of sex, but does not refer specifically to gender. Secondly, Article 1 states that sex discrimination exists if it 'has the purpose or effect' of impairing or nullifying the recognition, enjoyment or exercise by women ...of human rights and fundamental freedoms in the political, economic, social, cultural, civil or any other field.' The term 'purpose' implies intent, but the term 'effect' specifically does not.[153] Thirdly, Article 1 states that sex discrimination must be prohibited in the enjoyment of human rights and fundamental freedoms in the political, economic, social, cultural, civil or any other field. The latter is an open-ended formula extending coverage to all rights and areas of life. *CEDAW* therefore prohibits sex discrimination not just in the areas delineated by Articles 6–16 but in all other areas of women's lives.[154] Fourthly, to constitute discrimination, the distinction, exclusion or restriction made on the basis of sex must 'impair or nullify' a woman's rights. This means the distinction, exclusion or restriction must adversely affect her rights, broadly conceptualized. If it does not adversely affect her rights; '[a] sex-based action or practice which enhances women's enjoyment of their rights and freedoms is not discrimination against them within the meaning of the Convention.'[155]

The *CEDAW* Committee has developed an extensive jurisprudence on sex discrimination through its General Recommendations, concluding observations and through its communications and inquiry procedures established under the Optional Protocol, enabling the *CEDAW* Committee to interpret and apply the norms of *CEDAW* to concrete controversies.[156] The *CEDAW* Committee

152 Rikki Holtmaat, 'The CEDAW: A Holistic Approach to Women's Equality and Freedom' in Anne Hellum and Henriette Aasen (eds.), *Women's Human Rights. CEDAW in International, Regional and National Law* (Cambridge University Press, 2013), 95–124: 97.

153 Simone Cusack and Lisa Pusey, '*CEDAW* and the Rights to Non-Discrimination and Equality' *Melbourne Journal of International Law* 14 (2013), 54–92: 60–62.

154 Debrovka Simonovich, 'Global and Regional Standards on Violence against Women: The Evolution and Synergy of the CEDAW and Istanbul Conventions' *Human Rights Quarterly* 36 (2014), 590–607: 599.

155 Andrew Byrnes, 'Article 1' in Marsha Freeman, Christine Chinkin and Beate Rudolf (eds.), *The UN Convention on the Elimination of All Forms of Discrimination against Women: A Commentary* (Oxford University Press, 2012), 60.

156 Druscilla Scribner and Tracy Slagter, 'Recursive Norm Development: The Role of the Supranational Courts' *Global Policy* 8(3) (2017), 322–332: 325.

receives and considers communications from 'individuals or groups of individuals who claim to be victims of violations of rights set forth in the Convention, or by their designated representatives, or by others on behalf of an alleged victim where the alleged victim consents.'[157] The number of communications received has grown steadily since the Optional Protocol entered into force. To date in 2020 it has received 139 complaints, with 39 ruled inadmissible, 56 pending, and 33 final Views published, five of which were unsuccessful.[158] It has also published five Inquiry Reports resulting from its power to investigate 'grave or systematic violations' of women's rights.[159]

In each inquiry completed, the Committee has found multiple examples of sex discrimination in violation of *CEDAW*. In the first inquiry, the Committee examined Mexico's failure to protect women against widespread abduction, rape and murder in and around Ciudad Juárez and concluded Mexico had violated several provisions of *CEDAW*.[160] In particular, the Committee noted that 'the obligation to eliminate discrimination against women refers not only to actions or omissions by the State at all levels, but also to the need to take all appropriate measures to eliminate discrimination against women by any person, organization or enterprise.'[161] In the second inquiry, the Committee examined the extremely high levels of violence against aboriginal women and girls in Canada.[162] The Committee found multiple acts of sex discrimination by the state, including intersectional discrimination. It noted that violence against women is a form of sex discrimination.[163] In the third inquiry, the Committee examined an Executive Order which had the effect of banning artificial contraceptives in the city of Manila in the Philippines.[164] The Committee stated that the:

157 *Optional Protocol to the Convention on the Elimination of all Forms of Discrimination against Women* 1999, Article 1.

158 Office of the High Commissioner, https://www.ohchr.org/en/hrbodies/cedaw/pages/cedawindex.aspx.

159 Optional Protocol, above n. 157, Article 8.

160 *Report of the Inquiry concerning Mexico produced by the Committee on the Elimination of Discrimination against Women under article 8 of the Optional Protocol to the Convention* 27 January 2005.

161 *Ibid.*, at para 264.

162 *Report of the Inquiry concerning Canada of the Committee on the Elimination of Discrimination against Women under article 8 of the Optional Protocol to the Convention* 30 March 2015.

163 *Ibid.*, at paras 197, 200, 213–215.

164 *Report of the Inquiry concerning the Philippines of the Committee on the Elimination of Discrimination against Women under article 8 of the Optional Protocol to the Convention* August 2014.

> [D]enial of access to affordable sexual and reproductive health services, including the full range of methods of contraception, had severe consequences not only for the lives and health of many women, but also impacted on their enjoyment of several rights set forth in the Convention in areas such as employment and education.[165]

In the fourth inquiry, the Committee examined the abortion laws of the United Kingdom and Northern Ireland.[166] The Committee found that the laws perpetrated multiple acts of sex discrimination, including preventing women from exercising reproductive choice, causing mental or physical suffering constituting violence against women[167] and hindering women's access to sexual and reproductive health services.[168] Finally, in the fifth inquiry, the CEDAW Committee examined bride kidnappings in the Kyrgyz Republic and found that the Republic had failed to prevent, protect and assist victims, as well as to prosecute and adequately punish perpetrators.[169] Discrimination occurs, the CEDAW Committee explained, not only through the failure of states to take the necessary legislative measures but also through failing to enforce existing laws.[170]

The CEDAW Committee has issued 37 General Recommendations. Of these, General Recommendation No. 28 on Article 2 provides the most detailed guidance on sex discrimination clarifying its scope and setting out how to determine when and whether there is sex discrimination. Each pertinent point identified in this General Recommendation is individually examined below in light of the CEDAW Committee's responses in its Views, its Inquiry reports and in its concluding observations to individual states parties.

General Recommendation No. 28 states that 'although the Convention only refers to sex-based discrimination' Article 1 when viewed together with Articles 2(f) and 5(a) indicates that CEDAW also prohibits 'gender-based discrimination against women'.[171] The extension of sex discrimination to encom-

165 *Ibid.*, at para 47.

166 *Report of the Inquiry concerning the United Kingdom of Great Britain and Northern Ireland of the Committee on the Elimination of Discrimination against Women under article 8 of the Optional Protocol to the Convention* 23 February 2018.

167 *Ibid.*, at para 66.

168 *Ibid.*, at para 72.

169 *Report of the Inquiry concerning Kyrgyz Republic of the Convention on the Elimination of All Forms of Discrimination against Women under article 8 of the Optional Protocol* 23 February 2018.

170 *Ibid.*, at para 20 (b) and (c).

171 CEDAW Committee, *General Recommendation No. 28, on the Core Obligations of States Parties under Article 2 of the Convention on the Elimination of All Forms of Discrimination against Women* 16 December 2010 47th Session, at para 5.

pass gender discrimination is made in numerous forums by the CEDAW Committee, and it is clear that whether the discrimination is grounded in biological difference or gender difference both violate CEDAW.[172]

The General Recommendation defines the phrase 'effect or purpose' as meaning that it is sex discrimination 'even where discrimination was not intended.'[173] This makes clear that intent is not relevant to determining sex discrimination. Indeed, the CEDAW Committee does not refer to any requirement for intent to discriminate in any of its published Views.[174] In its Inquiry Report on abortion law in the United Kingdom and Northern Ireland, the Committee confirms that the Convention 'deliberately adopts a dual "effect" and "purpose" approach in order to capture acts that might have a discriminatory effect even when not intentional.'[175]

The General Recommendation also articulates that not only must states parties themselves refrain from sex discrimination but 'they are further obliged to react actively against discrimination against women, regardless of whether such acts or omissions are perpetrated by the State or by private actors.'[176] The CEDAW Committee has noted in its published Views, many of which focus on violence against women by non-state actors, that the state must act with due diligence to prevent violence against women and to investigate and punish acts of violence and provide protective services and compensation to the victims.[177] In further support of the due diligence principle, the CEDAW Committee found in its 2018 Inquiry Report on bride kidnapping and forced marriages in the Krygz Republic that multiple failures of due diligence had been borne by the state.[178] Bride-kidnapping involves choosing a victim, who is abducted, usually with the help of family members or friends. She is brought by force to the house of the kidnapper's parents, where preparations for a traditional wedding ceremony are under way.[179] She is pressured to consent to the marriage, and,

---

172 Dianne Otto, 'International Human Rights Law: Towards Rethinking Sex/Gender Dualism' in Vanessa Munro and Margaret Davies (eds.), *The Ashgate Research Companion to Feminist Legal Theory* (Routledge, 2013), 197–216: 204, 205.

173 General Recommendation 28, above n. 171, at para 5.

174 Bistra Netkova, 'Gender and the Right to Non-discrimination in International Human Rights Law' *Journal of Liberty and International Affairs* 1(3) (2016), 20–29: 25.

175 Inquiry concerning the United Kingdom of Great Britain and Northern Ireland, above n. 166, at para 65.

176 General Recommendation 28, above n. 171, at para 10.

177 Dubravka Simonovic, 'Global and Regional Standards on Violence against Women: The Evolution and Synergy of the CEDAW and Istanbul Conventions' *Human Rights Quarterly* (2014), 590–606: 600.

178 Inquiry concerning Kyrgyz Republic, above n. 169, at para 26.

179 *Ibid.*

sometimes assisted by her parents who wish to avoid the stigma attached to victims who escape forced marriage, she complies.[180] Due diligence, although the practice of bride kidnapping occurs entirely in the private context of family, requires the state to effectively investigate, prosecute and punish cases of bride kidnapping and related sexual violence.[181] It also entails that states parties must provide protective orders for victims,[182] criminalize marital rape[183] and to provide mandatory, systematic and effective capacity-building for the judiciary and law enforcement bodies on the strict application of legislation prohibiting these crimes.[184] The Committee found many *CEDAW* violations but specifically noted that states parties must 'react actively against discrimination against women, regardless of whether such acts or omissions are perpetrated by the State or by private actors.'[185]

General Recommendation No. 28 mandates that both direct and indirect discrimination must be prohibited.[186] This is in accord with many of the concluding observations of the *CEDAW* Committee in which it repeatedly directs states parties to incorporate into their legislation 'a comprehensive definition of discrimination against women and girls in line with article 1 of the Convention, encompassing direct and indirect discrimination'.[187] While cases of direct discrimination are often straightforward, causation has prevented claims from success in some instances.[188] For example in *Nguyen v. The Netherlands*,[189] the author was working in two part-time positions and making payments into a separate insurance scheme for each job. She applied for maternity leave

180 Lori Handrahan, 'Hunting for Women: Bride-Kidnapping in Kyrgyzstan' *International Feminist Journal of Politics* 6(2) (2004), 207–233; Noor O'Neill Borbieva, 'Kidnapping Women: Discourses of Emotion and Social Change in the Kyrgyz Republic' *Anthropological Quarterly* (2012), 141–169; and Russell Kleinbach and Gazbubu Babaiarova, 'Reducing Non-Consensual Bride Kidnapping in Kyrgyzstan' *Eurasian Journal of Social Sciences* 1(1) (2013), 50–60.

181 Inquiry concerning Kyrgyz Republic, above n. 169, at para 57.

182 *Ibid.*, at para 63.

183 *Ibid.*, at para 61, 62.

184 *Ibid.*, at para 70 (c).

185 *Ibid.*, at para 55.

186 General Recommendation No. 28, above n. 171, at para 16.

187 Simon Forshaw, 'Direct and Indirect Discrimination: Is There Something In Between?' *Indiana Law Journal* 37(4) (2008), 347–364: 348, 351.

188 Concluding Observations of the *CEDAW* Committee: Antigua and Barbuda (March 2019), at para [18] (Un Doc CEDAW/C/ATG/CO/4–7); Qatar (July 2019), at para [13(b)] (UN Doc CEDAW/QAT/CO/2); and Mozambique (July 2019), at para [12] (UN Doc CEDAW/MOZ/CO/3–5).

189 *Dung Thi Thuy Nguyen v. The Netherlands* Communication No. 3/2004, UN Doc. CEDAW/C/36/D/3/2004 CEDAW Committee (29 August 2006).

under both insurance schemes and was denied payment under one scheme due to an anti-accumulation clause which only allows (in cases of concurrent claims for maternity benefits) payment of benefits that exceed the benefits payable under another scheme. If she had one full time job, then she would have been entitled to the equivalent of the total amount of the two smaller payments from the two schemes.[190] Nguyen argued it was direct sex discrimination because 'only women are affected negatively by a loss of income that can never be experienced by men. That loss of income – an effect of the Act – constitutes discrimination.'[191] The majority opinion of the Committee held that the discrimination she experienced was not caused by her sex but by her dual employment status and, hence, there was no sex discrimination.[192] The Committee stated that the differential treatment was because she had two jobs – the first a salaried employee and the second a co-working spouse in her husband's enterprise – not because she was a woman.[193] The dissenting opinion found causation was established. Most part-time workers in the Netherlands are women and, compared to full-time employees, part-time workers are more likely to be employed in more than one position at the one time. A contractual clause that discriminates against dual employment status is discriminating on the ground of sex.[194]

Some commentators argue that although the Committee is very clear that sex discrimination does and must extent to indirect discrimination, it has struggled in its published Views to recognize indirect discrimination.[195] For example, in *G.D. and S.F. v. France*[196] the two authors were prevented by a customary rule from taking their mother's name. They argued this constituted sex discrimination, since Article 16(g) (on equality in family relations) guarantees the right to transmit a family name and, in combination with Article 1, that right must be free from sex discrimination.[197] G.D. was a 28-year-old unmarried teacher with no children. At birth, she was automatically given her father's last name, pursuant to a customary rule in force at the time, according

190 *Ibid.*, at para 2.2, 2.3, 2.6.

191 *Ibid.*, at para 3.1, 7.6.

192 *Ibid.*, at para 10.2.

193 *Ibid.*

194 *Ibid.*

195 Simone Cusack and Lisa Pusey, 'CEDAW and the Rights to Non-Discrimination and Equality' *Melbourne Journal of International Law* 14 (2013), 1–39; and Athena Nguyen, 'Through the Eyes of Women? The Jurisprudence of the CEDAW Committee' *Outskirts* 30 (2014), https://papers.ssrn.com/sol3/papers.cfm?abstract_id=2500545.

196 *G.D. and S.F. v. France* Communication No. 12/2007, UN Doc. CEDAW/C/44/D/12/2007 CEDAW Committee (4 August 2009).

197 *Ibid.*, at para 3.1.

to which a child born in a marriage must have the family name of the father. The author was raised exclusively by her mother and her mother's family after being abandoned by her father and his family.[198] The second author S.F. was a 39-year-old unmarried woman also with no children. At birth, like G.D. she was automatically given her father's family name, pursuant to the same customary rule. Although her father was originally living with her and her mother, he was violent and abandoned the family when she was very young.[199] While legislation has been subsequently enacted enabling a child to take a mother's name, it was not retroactive and gave the father a veto right allowing him to oppose the transmission of the mother's family name. France argued that the authors, because they are not married, and do not have children, cannot be victims of the violation of a right guaranteed in Article 16(g) CEDAW which specifically protects married women. The Committee agreed:

> The Committee therefore shares the view of the State party that since the authors are not married, do not live in husband-and-wife relationships and do not have children, they cannot be victims of a right whose beneficiaries are only married women, women living in de facto union or mothers.[200]

The Committee also went on to state that, as well as not being victims, it was satisfied 'that the authors have failed to show that they suffered any sex-based discrimination by bearing their father's family name' because the law regarding the transmission of the father's surname applied equally to male and female children.[201] In a strong dissenting opinion, six Committee members were collectively of the view that the authors were victims of indirect sex discrimination because the legislation was founded on a patriarchal view of fathers as heads of family imposed by the state party during their childhood.[202] The dissenting six further stated:

> The fact that such discrimination equally affected all children irrespective of their sex does not change the undisputed fact that the authors acquired a family name under a rule which is discriminatory, as it applies only against women's last names, thus amounting to a form of

198 *Ibid.*, at para 2.1.

199 *Ibid.*, at para 2.12.

200 *Ibid.*, at para 11.10.

201 *Ibid.*, at para 11.12.

202 *Ibid.*, at para 12.13 (Dubravka Šimonović, Yoko Hayashi, Ruth Halperin-Kaddari, Silvia Pimentel, Violeta Neubauer and Saisuree Chutikul).

> discrimination against women falling under articles 2, 5 and 16 of the Convention.[203]

Indeed, if a child cannot take a mother's name, that is a differentiation based on sex, regardless of whether the child is male or female. Additionally, the Committee's focus on Article 16(1)(g) and its wording in favour of only married women seems contrary to the position that CEDAW is a living document, and all areas of women's lives are protected from sex discrimination, not just those specifically identified. Similar to *Nguyen*, a more nuanced analysis that incorporated the concept of indirect discrimination was required to understand how sex discrimination was present in this case.[204]

General Recommendation No. 28 mandates that 'states parties must legally recognize intersecting forms of discrimination and their compounded negative impact on the women concerned and prohibit them.'[205] The Committee also repeatedly urges states parties to recognize 'intersecting forms of discrimination' in its concluding observations to different countries.[206] However, as with indirect discrimination (and in many of the same cases), the CEDAW Committee, despite its continual references to intersecting discriminations in its concluding comments, has itself missed opportunities to identify and highlight intersecting forms of discrimination.

In *Kayhan v. Turkey*,[207] the author was dismissed from her workplace for wearing a headscarf. Turkey argued that the regulations on workplace attire apply equally to male and female civil servants and both sexes face the same disciplinary and legal action should they not comply, and therefore, her dismissal does not discriminate against women and is not, therefore, sex discrimination.[208] The CEDAW Committee determined the complaint to be inadmissible because the author had failed to raise sex-based discrimination in the unsuccessful domestic proceedings that preceded her complaint to the CEDAW Committee. Instead, in the domestic proceedings she had argued

203 *Ibid.*, at para 12.6.

204 Susanne Zwingel, 'CEDAW as a "Living Document": Over Thirty Years of Committee Work' in *Translating International Women's Rights* (Palgrave MacMillan, 2016), 65–107.

205 General Recommendation 28, above n. 171, at para 18.

206 Concluding Observations of the CEDAW Committee: Antigua and Barbuda (March 2019), at para 18 (Un Doc CEDAW/C/ATG/CO/4–7); Concluding Observations of the CEDAW Committee: Seychelles (November 2019), at para 9] (Un Doc CEDAW/C/SYC/CO/46); and Concluding Observations of the CEDAW Committee: Guyana (July 2019), at para 14 (Un Doc CEDAW/C/GUY/CO/9).

207 *Rahime Kayhan v. Turkey* Communication No. 8/2005, UN Doc. CEDAW/C/34/D/8/2005 CEDAW Committee (3 February 2006).

208 *Ibid.*, at para 4.4.

breaches of the right to freedom of work, religion and thought; the right to be free from religious discrimination; and the right to physical and spiritual well-being.[209]

Many women who face multiple and intersecting discriminations find it difficult to determine the precise origin of the unfavourable treatment and the author herself may have been unsure of the exact cause of the discrimination. In fact, the dismissal was likely based on a range of intersecting factors all linked to her sex and the author's overall status as a 'Muslim woman'.[210] The headscarf is worn exclusively by women and any regulation which affects the wearing of the headscarf will have a disproportionate impact on women. As such, the unequal consequences of applying this seemingly gender-neutral rule would constitute indirect sex discrimination.

Similarly, in the following year in the case of *Zheng v. The Netherlands*[211] the author was a victim of child trafficking and had been held in sexual and domestic slavery in the Netherlands. The Committee found that as well as not exhausting domestic remedies, the author had not raised sex discrimination in her domestic proceedings and the communication was declared inadmissible.[212] The author was likely a victim of multiple forms of discrimination, including sex since sex trafficking is a gendered crime, but also youth, and socio-economic deprivation leading to illiteracy.[213] In dissent, three members of the Committee stated that the purpose of the communications procedure is to enable women:

> [t]o obtain the benefit of the law as intended and to take remedial action when domestic procedures have failed them. In the light of the nature of the crime of trafficking and the difficulty for victims, who are often uneducated and traumatized, to report precisely and with great details their experience, we are of the view that the Netherlands did not act with the due diligence that the author's situation required by failing to recognize

209 *Ibid.*, at para 7.6.

210 Nguyen, above n. 189; and Alda Facio, *The OP-CEDAW as a Mechanism for Implementing Women's Human Rights: An Analysis of the First Five Cases under the Communications Procedure of the OP-CEDAW* Occasional Papers Series No. 12 (International Women's Rights Action Watch Asia Pacific, 2008), 42.

211 *Zhen Zhen Zheng v. Netherlands* Communication No. 15/2007, UN Doc. CEDAW/C/42/D/15/2007 *CEDAW* Committee (27 October 2008).

212 *Ibid.*, at para 7.3.

213 Mary Burke, Barbara Amaya, and Kelly Dillon, 'Sex Trafficking as Structural Gender-Based Violence: Overview and Trauma Implications' in *The Palgrave International Handbook of Human Trafficking* (2020), 451–465; and Breezy Ferreira, 'A Global Crime Against Women: Sex Trafficking and Its Consequences' *Perspectives* 10(1) (2018), 1–14.

that she might have been a victim of trafficking in human beings and accordingly inform her of her rights.[214]

The approaches of the Committee in *Zheng* and in *Kayan* means that a victim must recognize that they are a victim of sex discrimination when pursuing domestic remedies and, in recognizing it as sex discrimination must pursue the claim in those terms regardless of whether it is an accessible avenue in their country and regardless of whether it has the potential for any positive outcome (noting that sex discrimination claims are often unsuccessful and the remedies weak).

More recently, the CEDAW Committee has more effectively recognized the complexities of intersectional discrimination.[215] In 2011 in *da Silva Pimentel v. Brazil*,[216] Pimentel, a 28-year-old Afro-Brazilian woman, died of complications resulting from her pregnancy after a health centre in Rio de Janeiro failed to provide appropriate and timely access to emergency obstetric care. Pimentel's death could have been prevented if the health centre had correctly diagnosed and treated her for intrauterine foetal death.[217] The authors argued the denial or neglect of health-care interventions that only women need is a form of sex discrimination against women in breach of Article 1 CEDAW coupled with Article 12 (the right to equality in health).[218] The Committee agreed.[219] It referred to its concluding observations to Brazil in 2007, where it had noted the existence of discrimination against women, especially women from the most vulnerable sectors of society such as women of African descent.[220] It also noted that such discrimination was exacerbated by regional, economic and social disparities.[221] The Committee referred to General Recommendation No. 28 specifically and its recognition that discrimination against women based on sex and gender is inextricably linked to other factors that affect women, such as race, ethnicity, religion or belief, health, status, age, class, caste,

214 *Zhen Zhen Zheng*, above n. 211, at para 8.7 (Mary Shanthi Dairiam, Violeta Neubauer and Silvia Pimentel).

215 Mpoki Mwakagali, 'International Human Rights Law and Discrimination Protection. A Comparison of Regional and National Responses' in *Comparative Discrimination Law Series* (Brill, 2017), 1–73: 16.

216 *Alyne da Silva Pimentel Teixeira v. Brazil* Communication No. 17/2008, UN Doc. CEDAW/C/49/D/17/2008 CEDAW Committee (25 July 2011).

217 *Ibid.*, at para 2.7, 2.8.

218 *Ibid.*, at para 3.1, 3.2, 3.5.

219 *Ibid.*, at para 7.5.

220 *Ibid.*, at para 7.7.

221 *Ibid.*

and sexual orientation and gender identity.[222] The Committee concluded that Pimentel was discriminated against, not only on the basis of her sex, but also on the basis of her status as a woman of African descent and her socio-economic background.[223]

In another example, in the case of *Kell v. Canada*,[224] the indigenous author was a victim of serious domestic violence over a period of years by her now deceased partner. The author had applied to purchase housing earmarked for the indigenous community. She was advised by the Housing Authority to apply for a family unit with her non-indigenous partner as her spouse, which meant she lost the opportunity to have sole title to the property.[225] Amongst other abuses, the author's violent partner subsequently convinced the Housing Authority to unlawfully remove her name from the title without her knowledge or consent.[226] This meant that housing designated for indigenous persons was now solely in the name of a non-indigenous person. Additionally, the removal of the author from the title put her partner in a powerful position culminating in him ejecting her and her children from the home. The author argued that the Canadian state allowed its agents (namely, the Northwest Territories Housing Corporation and the Rae-Edzo Housing Authority) to discriminate against her on the basis of her sex, marital status and cultural heritage, because it failed to ensure that its agents provide her with non-discriminatory treatment.[227]

Canada argued that the author did not raise any direct or indirect acts of discrimination as defined in Article 1 CEDAW in her domestic actions, perhaps inspired by *Kayan* and *Zhang*. The Committee in this case, however, did not reject the claim as inadmissible on that basis.[228] In finding for the author, the Committee, as in *Pimentel*, referred to General Recommendation No. 28 stating that discrimination against women based on sex and gender is inextricably linked to other factors that affect women, such as race, ethnicity, religion or belief, health, status, age, class, caste, and sexual orientation and gender identity.[229] The Committee concluded that as the author 'is an aboriginal woman who is in a vulnerable position, the State party is obliged to

---

222 *Ibid.*, at para 7.6.

223 *Ibid.*, at para 7.7.

224 *Cecilia Kell v. Canada* No. 19/2008, UN Doc. CEDAW/C/51/D/19/2008 CEDAW Committee (27 February 2012).

225 *Ibid.*, at para 2.2.

226 *Ibid.*, at para 2.5.

227 *Ibid.*, at para 3.1, 3.2.

228 *Ibid.*, at para 4.4, 7.3.

229 *Ibid.*, at para 10.2.

ensure the effective elimination of intersectional discrimination.'[230] In addition, in its Inquiry Report on violence against aboriginal women and girls in Canada,[231] the Committee noted that the different forms of violence experienced by aboriginal women and girls 'constitute multiple forms of discrimination against them based on their sex, gender and aboriginal identity' and that 'intersecting forms of discrimination and their combined negative impact on aboriginal women aggravate violence against aboriginal women.'[232] Hence, the CEDAW Committee has demonstrated in these instances a shift towards more nuanced analysis in cases of intersectional discrimination and toward an understanding of how sex discrimination may exist alongside and in addition to other forms of discrimination.

However, in contrast to the positive interpretations detailed above, the CEDAW Committee published in 2014 its Views in the case of *R.P.B. v. the Philippines*[233] where it failed to appreciate the intersectional discrimination at play. R.P.B. is deaf and mute. At age 17 she was raped by J. her 19-year-old neighbour in her residence. On the same day, she reported the rape to the police, and was interviewed by a male police officer, despite the law requiring such an interview be conducted by a female officer. The police officer drew up an affidavit in Filipino and asked her and her sister to countersign it, which she did although she did not understand it, as she was only able to read in English.[234] The medical examination of R.P.B. indicated 'clear evidence of recent history of blunt penetrating trauma to the labia minora and posterior fourchette'.[235] J. was arrested but at his subsequent trial he was acquitted. R.P.B. argued that the court process amounted to sex discrimination, firstly, because it failed to assess the evidence and apply the law properly and with due diligence; secondly, because it relied on gender-based myths and stereotypes (such as in the absence of torn clothing there can be no evidence of lack of consent and that in the absence of physical resistance her account is not credible); and thirdly, because it failed to consider the rape in the context of her vulnerability as a deaf girl.[236] The state failed to protect her from sex discrimination she argued,

230 *Ibid.*

231 *Report of the Inquiry concerning Canada of the Committee on the Elimination of Discrimination against Women under article 8 of the Optional Protocol to the Convention on the Elimination of All Forms of Discrimination against Women* UN Doc CEDAW/C/OP.8/CAN/1 (30 March 2015).

232 *Ibid.*, at para 204.

233 *R.P.B. v. the Philippines* No. 34/2011, UN Doc. CEDAW/C/57/D/34/2011 CEDAW Committee (21 February 2014).

234 *Ibid.*, at para 2.2.

235 *Ibid.*, at para 2.1.

236 *Ibid.*, at para 3.2, 3.3, 3.4.

in particular by not providing her, a woman who is deaf and mute, with accessibility to the court on an equal basis with other victims.[237]

The *CEDAW* Committee, in finding sex discrimination, stated that the Philippines had failed to guarantee her the effective protection against discrimination, particularly by not supplying an interpreter, as defined in Article 1 CEDAW, and within the meaning of its Article 2(c) and (d) read in conjunction with the Committee's General Recommendation No. 19.[238] Although a positive outcome, the reasoning does not make any comment on the intersections of discriminations faced by the author including age, gender and disability.

General Recommendation No. 28 takes up gender-based violence, noting that 'discrimination against women on the basis of sex and gender comprises, as stated in General Recommendation No. 19 on violence against women, gender-based violence, namely, violence that is directed against a woman because she is a woman or violence that affects women disproportionately.'[239] In contrast to some of the issues discussed above, the *CEDAW* Committee has consistently with respect to the issue of violence against women made findings that accord with General Recommendations Nos. 19, 28 and 35 in its Views and Inquiries.

In its first 2005 decision on violence against women, the *CEDAW* Committee explicitly stated that the failure to protect the author from domestic violence from her partner was sex discrimination.[240] The *CEDAW* Committee's Inquiry Report in Mexico also explicitly linked sex discrimination with the abduction, rape and murder of poor and young women.[241] Subsequently, the *CEDAW* Committee has confirmed gender-based violence is a form sex discrimination in many of its Views. In 2014, for example, in *Angela González Carreño v. Spain*,[242] the *CEDAW* Committee reaffirmed that gender-based violence is sex discrimination within the meaning of Article 1 of the Convention and that it is not limited to acts committed by or on behalf of governments. After a threat to her life from her husband, Carreño left the marital home, reported the facts to the police and applied for a trial separation.[243] The court granted care and custody of their daughter Andrea to Carreño but established a regime of

237 *Ibid.*, at para 3.8, 3.9.

238 *Ibid.*, at para 8.3.

239 *Ibid.*, at para 19.

240 *A.T. v. Hungary* No. 2/2003, UN Doc. CEDAW/C/32/D/2/2003 CEDAW Committee (26 January 2005).

241 Inquiry Report Mexico, above n. 160.

242 *Angela González Carreño v. Spain* No. 47/2012 UN Doc. CEDAW/C/58/D/47/2012 CEDAW Committee (16 July 2014).

243 *Ibid.*, at para 2.2.

unsupervised visits between father and daughter despite a request that visits be supervised. Andrea, seven years old, was murdered by her father during an unsupervised visit.[244] Carreño subsequently argued the state did not act 'with due diligence, with all means available to it and without delay to prevent, investigate, prosecute and punish the violence' against her and her daughter resulting in the murder of her daughter, and did not provide an effective judicial response or appropriate redress for the damages suffered for its negligence.[245]

Again in 2015, when the CEDAW Committee published its Views in the case of *X and Y v. Georgia*[246] it confirmed that gender-based violence is a form of sex discrimination.[247] Georgian nationals X and her daughter, Y argued the Georgia failed to protect them from domestic violence as required by its accession to CEDAW. X and her daughter Y from the age of 2, had been physically and sexually assaulted by X's husband, who was Y's father.[248] X was raped by him in 1987 and married him, believing that Georgian social and cultural norms defining virginity as essential to female virtue compelled her to marry him or to never marry. After ongoing violence, X complained to the police, but the prosecutor's office declined to open a criminal case and took no action beyond having her husband sign written pledges not to use violence to solve family disputes. The authors alleged (amongst other things) sex discrimination under Articles 1, 2(b)–(f) CEDAW (obligation of States Parties to adopt all appropriate measures to prevent discrimination).[249] In finding for X and Y, the Committee noted that sex discrimination includes gender-based violence against women and that it includes private acts if the state fails to act with due diligence to prevent violations of rights or to investigate and punish acts of violence and to provide compensation.[250]

Now that the delineations of the international human rights instruments taking up sex discrimination, ICCPR, ICESRC and CEDAW have been explored, the next part addresses their domestic applications in three countries, the United States, Australia and India.

244 *Ibid.*, at para 2.17.
245 *Ibid.*, at para 3.2.
246 *X and Y v. State of Georgia* No. 24/2009 UN Doc. CEDAW/C/61/D/24/2009 (2015).
247 *Ibid.*, at para 9.3.
248 *Ibid.*, at para 2.1, 2.2, 2.3.5.
249 *Ibid.*, at para 3.1.
250 *Ibid.*, at para 9.3.

Part 3: Translating International Sex Discrimination Law into Domestic Law

This part considers how the sex discrimination provisions of the *ICCPR*, *ICESCR* and *CEDAW*, and their interpretation by their respective treaty-bodies, have been translated into domestic law in three countries – the United States, Australia and India. Ratification, accession or succession to international conventions such as the *ICCPR*, *ICESCR* and *CEDAW* places an obligation on states parties to respect, protect and fulfil the rights contained within the conventions.[251] This includes, first, *de jure* obligations requiring the national laws of the state party to accord with the rights protected by the convention and, second, *de facto* obligations requiring that the protected rights are not merely reflected in the laws of the country but implemented in practice with the intended results.[252] This part focuses on *de jure* compliance, assessing the extent to which these three countries have replicated the approaches taken to sex discrimination claims by the three treaty-bodies in their national laws and their interpretation by the courts. In each of the three countries there are multiple avenues invoked to pursue sex discrimination claims. This part presents the most utilized avenue as illustrative examples of the operation of sex discrimination law in each country. The focus in the United States is on sex discrimination claims under Title VII of the *Civil Rights Act* 1964, in India on claims under section 15(1) of the *Constitution of India* 1950, and in Australia on claims under section 5 of the *Sex Discrimination Act* 1974.

In focusing on the translation of the sex discrimination protections provided by the *ICCPR*, *ICESCR* and *CEDAW* frameworks into three domestic law frameworks chosen for comparison, this part first considers the text of the selected sex discrimination law framework in each country. To meet the sex discrimination obligations of the *ICCPR*, *ICESCR* and *CEDAW*, states parties should include in their constitutions or legislation sex and/or gender as protected grounds of discrimination. The state parties should explicitly extend the prohibition on sex discrimination to encompass both direct and indirect discrimination and recognize the compounding effect of multiple discriminations. Sex

251 See the *Maastricht Guidelines on Violations of Economic, Social and Cultural Rights*, Maastricht, 1997, at para 6. http://www.escr-net.org/resources_more/resources_more_show.htm?doc_id=425803.

252 William T. Armaline, Davita Silfen Glasberg and Bandana Purkayastha, 'De Jure vs. De Facto Rights: A Response to "Human Rights: What the United States Might Learn from the Rest of the World and, Yes, from American Sociology' *Sociological Forum* 32(1) (2017), 220–224: 221.

discrimination should be prohibited by both the state and its representatives and private individuals and organizations in all areas of women's lives. After examining the texts of the sex discrimination protections, the part examines the interpretation of the legislative or constitutional text by the courts. The resulting jurisprudence provides a comparative platform to examine the varying approaches in the three country examples in determining whether sex discrimination has occurred. This includes considering the scope of sex as a discrimination ground, the elements for establishing direct and indirect discrimination, how causation is determined, whether an intent to discriminate on the ground of sex required, and finally whether differentiation on the basis of sex can be justified if 'reasonable', or in the employment context, as a business necessity.

3.1 *The Application of Sex Protection in the United States*

The United States, a federation of fifty states established by the *Constitution of the United States* 1789, is a party to the *ICCPR*.[253] It has signed but not acceded to *IESCR* and *CEDAW*.[254] Despite this failure to ratify significant relevant international conventions, the United States does have established avenues for pursuing sex discrimination claims. These include the equal protection guarantees of the Fourteenth and Fifth Constitutional Amendments,[255] the *Equal Pay Act* 1963,[256] and a raft of state-based legislation either mirroring or enhancing the federal protections.[257] The most-often used avenue and the focus of this section is Title VII of the 1964 *Civil Rights Act* (Title VII), the first comprehensive national anti-discrimination legislation enacted in the United States, and which provides the most substantial avenue of redress for victims of sex discrimination. The focus of the *Civil Rights Act* and its primary motivation for enactment was the African-American struggle for equality.[258] Indeed, sex as a protected ground was a last minute addition to the legislation,[259] after strong lobbying from women's groups, and it was narrowly introduced in the field of

---

253 The United States ratified the *ICCPR* on September 8, 1992.

254 Saleh Al Shraideh, 'CEDAW in the Eyes of the United States' *Journal of Legal Studies* 20(34) (2017), 18–37: 20.

255 Jody Feder, *Sex Discrimination and the United States Supreme Court: Developments in the Law* CRS Report RL 30253 (Congressional Research Service, 2015).

256 The *Equal Pay Act* 1963 prohibits sex discrimination in pay.

257 Since the enactment of the *Civil Rights Act* 1964 many states introduced their own sex discrimination protections primarily focused on employment discrimination.

258 Joni Hersch and Jennifer Shinall, 'Fifty Years Later. The Legacy of the Civil Rights Act of 1964' *Journal of Policy Analysis and Management* 34(2) (2015), 424–456: 429, 446.

259 Cary Franklin, 'Inventing the Traditional Concept of Sex Discrimination' *Harvard Law Review* 125 (2012), 1307–1380: 1318.

employment, initially excluding many other areas covered by the legislation, such as education and the delivery of services.[260] In 1972, however, the *Civil Rights Act* was amended to also extend sex discrimination protection in all education programs receiving funds from the Federal government.[261]

Title VII prohibits employers, public and private, with fifteen or more employees, from discriminating on the ground of sex in a range of employment practices.[262] It is unlawful to, on the ground of sex, 'fail or refuse to hire or to discharge any individual, or otherwise to discriminate against any individual with respect to his compensation, terms, conditions, or privileges of employment';[263] to 'limit, segregate, or classify' employees or applicants for employment in any way which would deprive or tend to 'deprive any individual of employment opportunities' or otherwise adversely affect their status as an employee, to discriminate against any individual 'in admission to, or employment in, any program established to provide apprenticeship or other training.'[264] Finally, it is unlawful 'to print or publish or cause to be printed or published any notice or advertisement relating to employment' indicating any preference, limitation, specification, or discrimination, based on sex.[265] The 1978 *Pregnancy Discrimination Act* inserted a new provision into Title VII expressly naming 'discrimination in employment on the basis of pregnancy, childbirth, or related medical conditions' as sex discrimination.[266] This amendment requires that employers treat 'women affected by pregnancy ... the same for all employment-related purposes ... as other persons not so affected but similar in their ability or inability to work.'[267]

Discrimination was not originally defined in the *Civil Rights Act* to explicitly include direct and indirect discrimination, but after judicial recognition of two forms of discrimination – disparate treatment and disparate impact – a new

260 Robert Bird, 'More Than a Congressional Joke: A Fresh Look, at the Legislative History of Sex Discrimination of the 1964 *Civil Rights Act*' *William and Mary Journal of Women and the Law* 3 (1997), 137–163: 161.

261 *Public Law No.* 92–318, 86 Stat. 235 1972.

262 *Civil Rights Act* 1964, Section 701. Title VII. It was expanded in 1972 to include public employers and reduced coverage of private employers from 25 employees to 15 employees for each working day in each of twenty or more calendar weeks in the current or preceding calendar year. *Public Law No.* 92–318, 86 Stat. 235 1972.

263 *Civil Rights Act* 1964, s. 703(a)(1).

264 *Civil Rights Act* 1964, s. 703(a)(2).

265 *Civil Rights Act* 1964, s. 704(b).

266 *Pregnancy Discrimination Act* 1978 Public Law 95–555. The amendment was a direct response to the Federal Courts finding in *General Electric Company v. Gilbert,* 429 U.S. 125 (1976).

267 *Ibid.*, s. 701(k) was added to the *Civil Rights Act* 1964.

section was inserted into Title VII to expressly provide for disparate impact as a particular form of employment discrimination.[268] Disparate treatment can be equated with direct discrimination while disparate impact can be equated (to some extent) with indirect discrimination.

The legislation provides a defence to sex discrimination where it is 'a bona fide occupational qualification reasonably necessary to the normal operation of that particular business or enterprise.'[269] Although the provisions that prohibit discrimination do not themselves identify intent as a necessary element, the remedies section states 'if the court finds that the respondent has intentionally engaged in or has intentionally engaged in an unlawful employment practice' the court may 'enjoin the respondent from engaging in such unlawful employment practice and order such affirmative action as may be appropriate' and award 'other equitable relief'.[270] This supported a requirement for intent to discriminate.

The next two sections below consider how the United States courts have interpreted Title VII in relation to sex discrimination based on the two forms of discrimination – disparate treatment and disparate impact – identified by the courts (and later incorporated into Title VII). Section 3.1.1 sets out and examines disparate treatment through the lens of a recent 2020 case, *Bostock v. Clayton County*.[271] Section 3.1.2 considers the expansion and subsequent retraction of disparate impact actions.

3.1.1 Disparate Treatment

Title VII prohibits discrimination in employment on the basis of sex in many aspects of employment, including hiring, firing, compensation, promotions, as well as the terms, conditions, or privileges of employment.[272] The court identified disparate treatment as the primary action flowing from Title VII, setting out the elements in the 1973 case of *McDonnell Douglas Corporation v. Green*,[273] which concerned sex discrimination in hiring practices. Disparate treatment firstly must concern a person who belongs to a protected class (for example, be of a particular sex or race). Secondly, the person must establish that she is qualified for the position (through her skills, education, and

268 *Civil Rights Act* 1991, *Public Law* 102–166.

269 *Civil Rights Act* 1964, s. 703(e)(1).

270 *Civil Rights Act* 1964, s. 706(g)(1).

271 *Bostock v. Clayton County*, 590 U.S. – (2020). Certiorari to the United States Courts of Appeals for the Eleventh Circuit No. 17–1618. Argued October 8, 2019—Decided June 15, 2020.

272 *Civil Rights Act* 1964, Title VII.

273 *McDonnell Douglas Corporation v. Green*, 411 U.S. 792 (1973).

experience). Thirdly, she must establish that, despite her qualifications, she suffered an adverse employment action (for example, she was not hired for the job) and finally that others similarly situated but not in the protected class were more favourably-treated (hired for the job). Once the person establishes these elements, the defendant can put forward a non-discriminatory reason for the alleged discriminatory action. If the defendant successfully proffers a reason, the burden shifts back to the person to show, if she can, that the employer's 'non-discriminatory' reason was merely a pretext for discriminatory behaviour.[274]

The elements of disparate treatment have evolved and developed since 1973, culminating in the 2020 case of *Bostock v. Clayton County*[275] where the Supreme Court held, for the first time, that discrimination on the ground of sex includes discrimination on the grounds of being same-sex attracted or transgender. *Bostock* involved three separate actions. Gerald Bostock, a county employee, was fired for 'unbecoming' conduct shortly after he began participating in a gay recreational softball league; Donald Zarda, who worked as a skydiving instructor, was fired after revealing he was gay; and Aimee Stephens, who presented as a male when she was originally hired six years earlier, was fired after she informed her employer that she planned to live and work full-time as a woman. The three former employees separately brought actions in different courts with different results and the three cases were heard together on appeal by the Supreme Court, which ruled 6–3 in favour of their petition.[276] This case, as well as expanding the meaning of sex, also neatly and clearly summarised the required elements for disparate treatment as they had evolved since the 1973 case of *McDonnell Douglas Corporation v. Green* as discussed below. These four elements, plus the defence of a bona fide occupational qualification, are reviewed in the following subsections.

3.1.1.1 *Opposite-Sex Comparator*

Title VII prohibits discrimination in various employment practices on the ground of sex. The majority in *Bostock* explained that the person bringing the action must belong to the protected class, in this case 'sex'. The employer defendants, the court explained, seek to define sex as a 'status as either male or female [as] determined by reproductive biology,' arguing this is the original meaning of Title VII when it was enacted in 1964. The early cases varied in their approach to defining sex. In some cases, the courts held that discrimination

274 *Ibid.*

275 *Bostock* above n. 271.

276 *Ibid.*

was not and could not be based on sex if there was no opposite-sex comparator. In other cases, the courts did not require an opposite-sex comparator. For example, in a series of actions against airlines that only employed female flight attendants, the court accepted that rules that terminated their contracts upon pregnancy or turning a certain age were sex discrimination despite the absence of an opposite-sex comparator.

A series of lower court cases also found that pregnancy discrimination was sex discrimination despite the lack of a male comparator.[277] However, the Supreme Court reversed the lower courts finding holding in 1974[278] and then again two years later in 1976[279] finding that pregnancy discrimination did not amount to sex discrimination because there was no (male) comparator. This led the court to conclude that 'an exclusion of pregnancy from a disability-benefits plan providing general coverage [was] not a gender-based discrimination at all.'[280] Congress shortly afterwards settled the issue in relation to pregnancy by enacting the *Pregnancy Discrimination Act* 1978 which modified Title VII's definition of sex to expressly include pregnancy-based distinctions. While the lack of an opposite-sex comparator can no longer prevent a pregnancy discrimination claim succeeding, breast-feeding, although intimately connected with pregnancy, has never succeeded also on the basis that is no male comparator. The court has stated: 'Drawing distinctions among women ... on the basis of their participation in breast-feeding activity, is simply is not the same as drawing distinctions between men and women. ... A prohibition against breast-feeding merely divides people into two groups (1) women who breast feed and (2) individuals who do not breast feed. ... Although the first group includes exclusively women and infants ... the second group includes members of both sexes.'[281]

Rules and policies around grooming and sex-based clothing have led to a series of cases where the courts have determined that the differences in policy and rules between men and women are not based on sex.[282] In these cases, however, a lack of an opposite-sex comparator was not the basis for the finding, since employers did clearly sort men and women into groups based on

277 *Dandridge v. Williams*, 397 U.S. 471 (1970).

278 *Geduldig v. Aiello*, 417 U.S. 484 (1974).

279 *General Electric Co. v. Gilbert*, 429 U.S. 125 (1976).

280 *Ibid.*

281 *Derungs v. Wal Mart Stores Inc.*, 141 F Supp. 884, 893 (SD Ohio 2000).

282 Mary Trautner and Samantha Kwan, 'Gendered Appearance Norms: An Analysis of Employment Discrimination Lawsuits, 1970–2008' *Gender and Sexuality in the Workplace* (2010), 127–150; and Meridith Harbach, 'Sexualization, Sex Discrimination, and Public School Dress Codes' *University of Richmond Law Review* (2015), 1039–1062.

their sex. Instead, the courts have never provided a clear rationale for dismissing these claims but have compared them to sex-segregated bathrooms and claimed that finding sex discrimination would have 'significant and sweeping implications.'[283] The requirement for an opposite-sex comparator, apart from the inconsistent approaches to the requirement depending on the issue and perspective adopted, inevitably excludes important forms of discrimination.

In *Bostock* an opposite-sex comparator approach was utilized but with an outcome different to the preceding cases. The employer-defendants argued that sex does not, and cannot, include the status of same-sex attracted or transgender.[284] Precedent supported them, although comparable to breast-feeding and grooming requirements, it is hard to differentiate same-sex attracted or transgender from pregnancy, marriage, motherhood and other characteristics which the court has accepted as integral to sex. In earlier cases, the courts had justified their selective application of the opposite-sex comparator requirement to determine sex on the basis that Congress likely did not intend 'to include all sexual distinctions in its prohibition of discrimination'.[285] The plaintiffs in *Bostock* argued that even in 1964, the term bore a broader scope, 'capturing more than anatomy and reaching at least some norms concerning gender identity and sexual orientation.'[286] While no previous cases had accepted that gender identity and sexual orientation were included in the status of sex, the courts had regularly recognized gender as a status included in sex. For example, ending a female's employment upon marriage is discrimination based on gender and not sex. In addition, numerous sex discrimination actions against airlines were based on gender and not sex. Female plaintiffs challenged rules used by airlines to require beautification and make-up for women (but not men) and uniforms for women (often impractical) such as miniskirts or 'hot pants and leather boots'.[287] Other discriminatory practices in the airlines were based gender-role stereotypes portraying women as 'icons of femininity' who are 'endlessly smiling, polite, caring and attractive' or as sex objects illustrated by advertising slogans such as National Airlines banner 'I'm Cheryl, Fly Me' in 1971.[288]

---

283 Burlette Carter, 'Sexism in the Bathroom Debates: How Bathrooms Really Became Separated by Sex' *Yale Law and Policy Review* 37 (2018), 227–297.

284 *Bostock*, above n. 271, at 5.

285 *Smith v. Liberty Mutual Insurance*, 569 Fd 325. See Franklin, above n. 259, at 1376.

286 *Bostock*, above n. 271, at 5.

287 Andrew Wilson, 'Boots, Indecency, and Secular Sacred Spaces: Implicit Religious Motives Underlying an Aspect of Airline Dress Codes' *Implicit Religion* 14(2) (2011), 173–192.

288 Tamilla Curtis and Blaise Waguespack, 'Case Study: Sexism in Advertising and Airlines' *Journal of Business Diversity* 15(1) (2015), 34–38.

The *Bostock* majority, in response to the question as to whether sex includes same-sex attracted or transgender status, stated that 'it is impossible to discriminate against a person for being homosexual or transgender without discriminating against that individual based on sex.'[289] In explaining this conclusion, the court utilized a simple opposite-sex comparator example. If a male employee is in a sexual relationship with another man and the employer is able to fire him because of that sexual relationship, yet unable to fire a woman employee in a relationship with the same man, then that is discrimination on the ground of sex. They concluded the 'individual employee's sex plays an unmistakable and impermissible role in the discharge decision.'[290]

The requirement that a person belong to a protected class, sex, seemingly simple, has not had a clear trajectory in the United States courts. Sex includes gender, however, rules and policies around grooming and dress codes (clearly gender-based differences) have been consistently excluded. Pregnancy, and (since *Bostock*) same-sex attraction and transgender status are sex differences, but breast-feeding is not. An opposite-sex comparator is sometimes, but not always, required.

3.1.1.2 *'Because of' Sex: Causation*

Title VII requires the discrimination to be because of 'such individual's … sex …'[291] This has given rise in the case-law to two elements – a requirement to establish whether the discrimination was caused by the ground of sex and a requirement to establish whether there was intent to discriminate on the ground of sex. Although these are clearly two separate questions, they are often linked in the cases. In *Bostock*, the defendants argued that any discrimination was not 'because of sex'.[292] They argued that if the court found sex discrimination (which it did), there was in addition discrimination on the basis of same-sex attraction and transgender status. Consequently, the defendants argued that it could not be said that any discrimination was merely 'because of' sex.[293]

The *Bostock* majority began by summarizing the meaning of the causation element. The court stated that the ordinary meaning of 'because of' is 'by reason of' or 'on account of.' 'In the language of law, this means that Title VII's "because of" test incorporates the "simple" and "traditional" standard of but-for causation.'[294] 'That form of causation is established whenever a particular

289 *Bostock*, above n. 271, at 9.
290 *Ibid.*, at 10.
291 *Civil Rights Act* 1964, Section 703(a)(1).
292 *Bostock*, above n. 271, at 15.
293 *Ibid.*
294 *Ibid.*, at 5.

outcome would not have happened "but for" the purported cause.'[295] The court further explained that: 'When it comes to Title VII, the adoption of the traditional but-for causation standard means a defendant cannot avoid liability just by citing some *other* factor that contributed to its challenged employment decision. So long as the plaintiff's sex was one but-for cause of that decision, that is enough to trigger the law.'[296] Finally, the court stated that if Congress intended that sex must be the only causative factor, they could have adopted the term 'solely' or 'primarily because of' but it did not. Instead, Congress amended Title VII in 1991 to allow a person to prevail merely by showing that a protected class like sex was a 'motivating factor' in a defendant's employment practice.[297] The court held that 'but for' the sex discrimination experienced by the three plaintiffs, the firings would not have occurred and therefore the 'but for' test is satisfied.[298] The court concluded:

> When an employer fires an employee because she is homosexual or transgender, two causal factors may be in play – *both* the individual's sex *and* something else (the sex to which the individual is attracted or with which the individual identifies). But Title VII doesn't care. If an employer would not have discharged an employee but for that individual's sex, the statute's causation standard is met, and liability may attach.[299]

From the earliest cases defendants argued (mostly unsuccessfully) that if there were other reasons for differentiation, alongside sex, then this would bring the claim outside of Title VII. In the 1971 case, *Phillips v. Martin Marietta*,[300] for example, the defendant company refused to hire women with young children and argued that it was motherhood and not sex that provided the reason for the differentiation. The defendant argued that excluding women with young children was not because they sought to exclude all groups of women, only those who were mothers, and therefore any discrimination was not 'because of sex'. The defendant was successful in the district court which found, based on gender-role stereotypes, that 'the responsibilities of men and women with small children are not the same and employers are entitled to recognize those different responsibilities in establishing hiring polices.'[301] The defendant was

---

295 *Ibid.*
296 *Ibid.*, at 6.
297 *Ibid.*
298 *Ibid.*, at 10.
299 *Ibid.*, at 11.
300 *Phillips v. Martin Marietta Corp.*, 411 F.2d 1 (5th Cir. 1969).
301 *Ibid.*

again successful in the Court of Appeal for the Fifth Circuit, but in the Supreme Court the plaintiff won.[302] The court asked 'but for' her sex would the differentiation have occurred. They found, firstly, that the plaintiff's sex was inextricably linked with motherhood and that if the plaintiff were a man with young children, the differentiation would not have occurred.[303] Further, the court stated that employers seldom have policies that exclude all women, rather they have policies that exclude particular women, in this case women with small children, and they cannot argue that it is not because of sex just because women who are not mothers are not impacted by the discriminatory policy.[304] Motherhood, the court stated, even if distinct from sex, does not remove an action from Title VII once sex is established as a cause of the differentiation.[305]

The series of cases brought by women working as flight attendants, arguing numerous forms of sex discrimination, against different airlines in the following years provides further examples.[306] Female flight attendants brought actions, for example, against American Airlines and Piedmont Aviation challenging two rules as sex discrimination. The first rule, embedded in the contracts of female flight attendants, authorized each employing airline to 'release' them within six months of marriage.[307] The second rule terminated employment when women reached the age of 33.[308] While American Airlines only hired female flight attendants, Piedmont Aviation employed both men and women.[309] Both airlines argued it was not sex discrimination to require women to leave when they married or when they turned 33 because they were differentiating between two groups of women – married and unmarried and young and old – and therefore the differentiation was not 'because of sex' but because of other factors. The Ninth Circuit rejected those arguments on the same basis as *Phillips*, that the presence of age and marriage discrimination did not invalidate a claim of sex discrimination.[310]

302 *Phillips v. Martin Marietta Corp.*, 400 U.S. 542 (1971) (No. 73).

303 *Ibid.*

304 *Ibid.*

305 *Ibid.* See Martha Chamallas, 'Mothers and Disparate Treatment: The Ghost of Martin Marietta' *Villanova Law Review* 44 (1999), 337–354: 342.

306 *Neal v. American Airlines, Inc.*, 605 F. Supp. 1145 (N.D. Ill. 1985); *Colvin v. Piedmont Aviation,* 1 CCH Employment Practices Guide 6003 (EEOC 1968); *Sprogis v. United Airlines*, 444 F.2d 1194 (7th Cir. 1971); and *Harris v. Pan American World Airways, Inc.*, 637 F.2d 1297, 1302 (9th Cir. 1980). See Roberta Lessor, 'Social Movements, the Occupational Arena and Changes in Career Consciousness: The Case of Women Flight Attendants' Journal of Occupational Behaviour 5(1) (1984), 37–51.

307 *Neal*, above n. 306.

308 *Ibid.*, at 306.

309 *Ibid.*

310 *Harris v. Pan American World Airways, Inc.*, 637 F.2d 1297, 1302 (9th Cir. 1980).

The argument that other causes should invalidate a sex discrimination action continued, despite its lack of success. Finally, however in the 1989 case, *Price Waterhouse v. Hopkins*,[311] the issue was firmly settled. Ann Hopkins had worked at Price Waterhouse for five years and after securing a $25 million government contract she was recommended for partnership by some of the partners. Of the 662 partners at the firm at that time, only seven were women and of the 88 persons proposed for partnership that year, the only woman was Hopkins. The Admissions Committee invited comments from the current partners on her proposal and 32 responded. Thirteen supported her bid for partnership. Three partners recommended that her candidacy be placed on hold, eight stated that they did not have an informed opinion about her, and eight recommended that she be denied partnership. While many praised her competence, supporters and opponents of her candidacy indicated 'that she was sometimes overly aggressive, unduly harsh, difficult to work with, and impatient with staff.'[312] One partner described her as 'macho', another that she 'overcompensated for being a woman' and a third advised her to take 'a course at charm school'.[313] Several partners criticized her use of profanity. The Policy Board decided to place her candidacy on hold, despite acknowledging she was qualified for partnership, and she was advised to 'walk more femininely, talk more femininely, dress more femininely, wear make-up, have her hair styled, and wear jewelry.'[314] The defendant argued that that the primary reason for their decision was her 'abrasive manner not her sex.'[315]

The court held that unless the plaintiff's interpersonal problems were the sole reason for denying her the partnership, and sex was not a contributing motive, sex discrimination could be found. The court concluded sex clearly was a motivating factor: 'It takes no special training to discern sex stereotyping in a description of an aggressive female employee as requiring "a course at charm school".'[316] Nor, does it require expertise in psychology to know that, 'if an employee's flawed interpersonal skills can be corrected by a soft-hued suit or a new shade of lipstick, perhaps it is the employee's sex, and not her interpersonal skills, that has drawn the criticism.'[317] It was not relevant therefore that her abrasive manner may also be a cause of the decision when sex clearly was one of the reasons they did not appoint her as a partner. The court held that in a mixed-motives case, the plaintiff has burden of proof as to sex and

311 *Price Waterhouse v. Hopkins*, 490 U.S. 228, 236 (1989).
312 *Ibid.*, at para 19.
313 *Ibid.*, at para 20.
314 *Ibid.*, at para 20.
315 *Ibid.*, at para 56.
316 *Ibid.*, at para 58.
317 *Ibid.*, at para 58.

the defendant has the burden of showing the causes of the differentiation are not sex related. The question to be determined through these different burdens is whether sex, when the employment decision was made, was a motivating factor.

After *Waterhouse,* the *Civil Rights Act* 1991 clarified the ruling in two ways. Firstly, the legislation provides that the burden shifts to the defendant once the plaintiff has established that sex was a 'motivating' factor for the discriminatory employment practice. Secondly, the legislation confirms that sex need only be a motivating factor, not a substantial factor as frequently argued by defendants.[318]

3.1.1.3 *Discrimination Must Be Intentional*

The wording in Title VII 'because of' has not only led to a causation requirement, but also a requirement of intent.[319] In order to show discriminatory intent, a plaintiff must demonstrate that the decision-maker selected or reaffirmed a particular course of action, at least in part 'because of', and not merely 'in spite of', its adverse effects on an identifiable group.'[320] The *Bostock* majority confirmed this position, stating: 'In so-called disparate treatment cases like today's, this court has also held that the difference in treatment based on sex must be intentional.'[321] 'Just as sex is necessarily a but-for cause when an employer discriminates against homosexual or transgender employees, an employer who discriminates on these grounds inescapably intends to rely on sex in its decision making.'[322] In this way, the Supreme Court, as have previous courts, links causation with intent.

Intent was not required in the earliest disparate treatment cases, however, it has become integral to a successful action as confirmed by the court in *Bostock.*[323] In many disparate treatment actions it is a challenging element because it can be hard to determine.[324] The courts have developed two approaches to establishing intent in disparate treatment cases. The first

---

318 For a discussion on the amendments, see Margaret Johnson, 'A Unified Approach to Causation in Disparate Treatment Cases: Using Sexual Harassment by Supervisors as the Causal Nexus for the Discriminatory Motivating Factor in Mixed Motive Cases' *Wisconsin Law Review* (1993), 231–259: 237.

319 *Civil Rights Act* 1964, s. 703(a)(1).

320 *Personnel Administrator of Mass v. Feeney*, 442 U.S. 256 (1979).

321 *Bostock*, above n. 271.

322 *Ibid.*

323 *Ibid.*

324 *McDonnell Douglas Corp. v. Green*, 411 U.S. 792, 802 (1973). See Joseph Seiner, 'Disentangling Disparate Impact and Disparate Treatment: Adapting the Canadian Approach' *Yale Law and Policy* 25(95) (2006), 95–142: 105.

is discerning intent from facts that require no inference. For example, the courts have held an explicit policy prohibiting employment of women with pre-school age children but not men, directly established intent;[325] that refusing to employ women as correctional officers in some (but not all) circumstances where men were employed directly established intent;[326] and that an employer's dress code requiring its female employees to wear a uniform as a condition of employment, while only requiring male employees in the same job position to wear 'appropriate business attire', directly established intent.[327]

Acknowledging that such overtly discriminatory statements or policies of discrimination are rare, the second approach to establishing intent is through circumstantial evidence. In the case of *Troupe v. May Department Stores Co.*,[328] the plaintiff was employed as a salesperson in a women's accessories department. She had begun working there in 1987, initially working part-time, but from July 1990 she worked full-time. Until the end of 1990 her work was entirely satisfactory. In December of that year, during the first trimester of her pregnancy, she began experiencing severe morning sickness. The following month she requested and was granted a return to part-time status, working from noon to 5:00 p.m. However, she continued to experience severe morning sickness causing her to be late to work on more than eleven occasions.[329] The day before her maternity leave was due to commence, she was fired for 'excessive tardiness'.[330] She argued that she was fired because the company did not want to pay her maternity benefits, and this constituted 'disparate treatment' on the ground of sex.[331] There was no direct evidence of intent to discriminate on the ground of sex as the defendant insisted she was fired for her tardiness and not because they did not want to pay her maternity benefits.[332] She therefore had to show through inference that disparate treatment based on sex

325 *Phillips v. Martin Marietta Corp.*, 400 U.S. 542 (1971).

326 *Harden v. Dayton Human Rehabilitation Centre*, 520 F. Supp. 769 (S.D. Ohio 1981); and *Griffin v. Michigan Department of Corrections*, 654 F. Supp. 690 (E.D. Michigan 1982). Note however that in *Dothard v. Rawlinson*, 433 U.S. 321 (1977), the court held that positions in the conditions of the Alabama prison would pose a substantial security problem directly linked to the sex of the prison guard. Furthermore, the court believed there was a likelihood that inmates would assault a woman simply because she was a woman. See Mary Farkas and Kathryn Rand, 'Female Correctional Officers and Prisoner Privacy' *Marquette Law Review* 80(4) (1997), 995–1030: 998.

327 *Carroll v. Talman Federal Savings & Loan Association*, 448 F. Supp. 79 (N.D. Ill. 1978).

328 *Troupe v. May Department Stores Co.*, 20 F. 3d 734 (7th Cir. 1994).

329 *Ibid.*, at para 2.

330 *Ibid.*, at para 2.

331 *Ibid.*, at para 2.

332 *Ibid.*, at para 6.

had occurred. According to the court, circumstantial evidence might include 'suspicious timing' or an 'ambiguous statement' or evidence that a similarly-situated person got better treatment.[333] Despite the very 'suspicious timing', the court denied her claim on the basis that she did not establish sufficient circumstantial evidence of an intent to discriminate.[334] The court noted that if the plaintiff had presented evidence of a similarly-situated person treated differently, she might have succeeded. The court stated: 'We doubt that finding a comparison group would be that difficult. Troupe would be halfway home if she could find one non-pregnant employee of Lord and Taylor who had not been fired when about to begin a leave similar in length to hers. She either did not look or did not find. Given the absence of other evidence, her failure to present any comparison evidence doomed her case.'[335]

In *Price Waterhouse v. Hopkins*,[336] the facts might have supported a finding of a direct intent to discriminate based on the discriminatory comments of the Policy Board to 'walk more femininely, talk more femininely, dress more femininely, wear make-up, have her hair styled, and wear jewelry.'[337] Justice Brennan explained that by 'motive' in a sex discrimination case, the court meant that, 'if we asked the employer at the moment of the decision what its reasons were and if we received a truthful response, one of those reasons would be that the applicant or employee was a woman.[338]

In the 2017 case, *Stephanie Hicks v. City of Tuscaloosa, Alabama*,[339] the plaintiff successfully argued disparate treatment in relation to discriminatory treatment in relation to work conditions that jeopardized her ability to breastfeed. After returning from maternity leave the plaintiff was placed on an assignment that required her to wear a bullet proof vest. Hicks's physician had advised that wearing the restrictive vest would put her at risk for breast infection and jeopardize her milk supply due to the pressure it would place on her breasts. Although her co-workers, who had non-breastfeeding-related medical restrictions, were regularly given temporary desk jobs, Hicks was forced off the police force.[340] The plaintiff argued that the defendant's proffered options – patrolling without a vest or patrolling with an ineffective larger vest – made work conditions so intolerable that any reasonable person would have been

333 *Ibid.*, at para 6.
334 *Ibid.*, at para 12.
335 *Ibid.*, at para 12.
336 *Price Waterhouse v. Hopkins*, above n. 311.
337 *Ibid.*, at para 139.
338 *Ibid.*, at para 141.
339 *Hicks v. City of Tuscaloosa, Alabama*, 870 F.3d 1253, 1253 (11th Cir. 2017).
340 *Ibid.*, at 1–6.

compelled to resign and that this sufficed to establish intention to discriminate.[341] The court agreed.[342]

3.1.1.4 *Discrimination Must Be against an Individual*

Title VII clearly specifies that sex discrimination is prohibited against individuals. Employers may not fail or refuse to hire or … discharge any *individual*, or otherwise … discriminate against any *individual* with respect to his compensation, terms, conditions, or privileges of employment, because of such *individual's* … sex (italics added).[343] The defendants in *Bostock* argued that they treated men and women similarly because they would fire any person if they were same-sex attracted or transgender. The majority of the court responded: 'On that understanding, the statute would require us to consider the employer's treatment of groups rather than individuals, to see how a policy affects one sex as a whole versus the other as a whole. That idea holds some intuitive appeal.'[344] However, despite that 'intuitive appeal' they rejected that argument on the basis that the meaning of the term 'individual' used in the text, is 'as uncontroversial in 1964 as it is today.'[345] Instead, they held that the legislation refers to '[a] particular being as distinguished from a class, species, or collection':

> Suppose an employer fires a woman for refusing his sexual advances. It is no defence for the employer to note that, while he treated that individual woman worse than he would have treated a man, he gives preferential treatment to female employees overall. The employer is liable for treating *this* woman worse in part because of her sex. Nor is it a defence for an employer to say it discriminates against both men and women because of sex. This statute works to protect individuals of both sexes from discrimination and does so.[346]

This finding confirms earlier decisions. In the 1978 case, *Los Angeles Dept. of Water and Power v. Manhart*,[347] an employer-defendant who required women to make larger pension fund contributions than men argued it was not sex discrimination because actuarial tables indicated women, as a class, lived longer

341 *Ibid.*, at 6–7, 9.

342 *Ibid.*, at 13.

343 *Civil Rights Act* 1964, s. 703(1).

344 *Bostock* above n. 271, 7.

345 *Bostock* above n. 271, 8.

346 *Bostock* above n. 271, 8.

347 *Los Angeles Dept. of* Water *and Power v. Manhart*, 435 U.S. 702 (1978), at 707–708.

than men and thus are likely to receive more from the pension fund over time. The court held, however, that disparate treatment discrimination must be determined at the individual level. and an individual woman could die as early as an individual man. The fact that overall men die earlier than women was irrelevant:

> The statute's focus on the individual is unambiguous. It precludes treatment of individuals as simply components of a racial, religious, sexual, or national class. If height is required for a job, a tall woman may not be refused employment merely because, on the average, women are too short. Even a true generalization about the class is an insufficient reason for disqualifying an individual to whom the generalization does not apply.[348]

3.1.1.5 *Bona Fide Occupational Qualification*

Title VII provides a defence for an employer who can show the sex discrimination is a 'bona fide occupational qualification reasonably necessary to the normal operation of that particular business or enterprise.'[349] As with all defences, the onus of proof is on the defendant. The courts have developed two elements to establishing the defence. The first is that the sex discrimination is necessary to the 'essence of the business' and the second is that 'all or substantially all' of a particular sex could not meet the qualification necessary.

These two tests are illustrated in the cases. In the 1967 case of *Weeks v. Southern Bell Telephone and Telegraph Co.*,[350] the female plaintiff was denied a switchman position that she was otherwise qualified for because the state code prohibited women from doing jobs that required lifting in excess of thirty pounds. The position was instead given to a male applicant of lesser seniority despite a company policy of seniority-based promotion. The plaintiff sued for unlawful sex discrimination under Title VII, and the defendant raised the defence of bona fide occupational qualification. The defendant argued that 'the duties of a switchman were so strenuous that all, or substantially all, women would be unable to perform them.'[351] The Fifth Circuit held that raising a stereotype of women as being unable to physically do the job could not

348 *Ibid.*, at 708.

349 *Civil Rights Act* 1964, s. 703.

350 *Weeks v. Southern Bell Telephone* & Telegraph *Co.*, 408 F. 2d 228 (5th Cir. 1969).

351 *Ibid.*, at para 41.

support the defence. Ultimately, the court concluded that a broad interpretation of the defence would result in the 'exception ... swallow[ing] the rule.'[352]

In the 1971 case of *Diaz v. Pan American World Airways*,[353] a group of male plaintiffs brought a claim against Pan Am challenging its policy of hiring only female flight attendants.[354] Pan Am agreed that the policy was sex discrimination but raised the defence of bona fide occupational qualification. The defendants argued that women were better suited to meet the 'psychological needs' of customers and more proficient at the 'non-mechanical aspects' of the job. According to the defendant the 'non-mechanical aspects' of the flight attendant position included 'providing reassurance to anxious passengers, giving courteous personalized service and, in general, making flights as pleasurable as possible within the limitations imposed by aircraft operations.'[355] The Fifth Circuit did not accept that these tasks represented the 'essence' of the business of the airline. Instead, the court stated that the airlines 'primary function ... is to transport passengers safely from one point to another' not to provide soothing flight attendants.[356] In addition, the court held that the defendant had not satisfied the first test that 'all or substantially all men could not adequately perform the tasks necessary to the airline's normal operation.'[357]

In the 1977 case of *Dothard v. Rawlinson*,[358] the Supreme Court found that a new regulation requiring prison guards to be the same sex as the inmates was lawful because sex was essential for the position. In support of its decision, the court noted that the 'essence' of the job is to maintain prison security.[359]

---

352 *Ibid.*, at para 51.

353 *Diaz v. Pan American World Airways*, 442 F. 2d 385 (5th Cir. 1971).

354 *Ibid.* See for a discussion of *Diaz* Rachel Martin, 'Barenaked Ladies and the Bona Fide Occupational Qualification: The Intersection of Gender and Privacy in Permissible Sex Discrimination' *Cumberland Law Review* 43 (2012), 495–528.

355 *Diaz*, above n. 353, at para 387.

356 *Diaz*, above n. 353.

357 *Diaz*, above n. 353; see also *Wilson v. Southwest Airlines Co.*, 517 F. Supp. 292, 293 n. 1 (N.D. Tex. 1981) where one hundred men sued Southwest Airlines for refusing to hire them. The defendant argued that 'femininity, or more accurately female sex appeal, was a bona fide occupational qualification ... for the jobs of flight attendant and ticket agent According to the defendant, 'attractive female flight attendants and ticket agents personified the airline's sexy image and fulfilled its public promise to take passengers skyward.' 'Slim, attractive, unmarried' women who are 'available' for the male passengers are crucial to their profitability. See Christine Williams and Catherine Connell, 'Looking Good and Sounding Right' Work and Occupations 37(3) (2010), 349–377; and Kathleen Barry, Femininity in Flight: A History of Flight Attendants (Duke University Press, 2007).

358 *Dothard v. Rawlinson*, 433 U.S. 321 (1977).

359 *Ibid.*

A female working in Alabama's dormitory-style prisons, in which inmates were not divided by severity of crime, would be constantly exposed to sex offenders and other inmates who were 'deprived of a normal heterosexual environment' in addition to general prison violence. A female guard's 'very womanhood would ... directly undermine ... the security that is the essence' of the correctional facility.[360] In addition, the court held that substantially all women would be unable to do the job because their very presence 'would pose a real threat not only to the victim ... but also to the basic control of the penitentiary and protection of its inmates and the other security personnel.'[361]

The Supreme Court addressed a different aspect of the 'essence of the business' test in the 1990 case of *International Union v. Johnson Controls.*[362] The defendant, a battery manufacturer, established a policy prohibiting all women (except those whose infertility had been medically documented) from working in positions requiring exposure to lead. A group of plaintiffs, both male and female, brought a class action arguing that the policy constituted sex discrimination.[363] The defendant argued it was a bona fide occupational qualification reasonably necessary to their normal operation because safety, including to foetuses, was essential to their business.[364] At first instance, the federal district court agreed finding that 'industrial safety' is part of the essence of the defendant's business, and that the foetal protection policy is reasonably necessary to further that concern.[365] The Supreme Court, however, held that the policy discriminated on the basis of sex and childbearing ability, as opposed to fertility, particularly since there was evidence in the record indicating the negative effects of lead on the male reproductive system.[366] The court held that the foetal-protection policy was not indispensable to the particular business and the defendant had presented no facts indicating that all or most women would be unable to 'safely and efficiently' make batteries.[367]

360 *Ibid.*
361 *Ibid.*
362 *United Automobile Workers v. Johnson Controls, Inc.*, 499 U.S. 187 (1991); and *International Union v. Johnson Controls*, 680 F. Supp. 309 (E.D. Wis. 1988).
363 *United Automobile Workers v. Johnson Controls, Inc.*, 499 U.S. 187 (1991).
364 *Ibid.*
365 *International Union v. Johnson Controls*, 680 F. Supp. 309 (E.D. Wis. 1988).
366 *United Automobile Workers v. Johnson Controls, Inc.*, 499 U.S. 187 (1991).
367 *Ibid.*

3.1.2 Disparate Impact

Title VII did not expressly prohibit indirect discrimination in its original enactment.[368] The Supreme Court, however, embraced the concept of disparate impact as distinct from disparate treatment in the case of *Griggs v. Duke Power Co* in 1971.[369] This was a race discrimination case in which a rule required employees who were transferring between different departments to have a high-school diploma or pass an intelligence test. African-American employees argued that those requirements did not measure a person's ability to perform a job or category of jobs. Instead, the rule resulted in race discrimination against them as African-American employees, who overwhelmingly did not meet the educational criteria. The court stated that 'good intent or absence of discriminatory intent does not redeem employment procedures or testing mechanisms that operate as built-in headwinds for minority groups and are unrelated to measuring job capability.' The court went on to state that 'facially neutral practices – even those not motivated by discriminatory intent or animus – may nonetheless contravene Title VII, if, in effect, they work to arbitrarily exclude protected classes at disproportionate rates.' The court concluded that Title VII 'proscribes not only overt discrimination but also practices that are fair in form but discriminatory in operation'[370] The concept of indirect discrimination aligns with this initial demarcation.[371]

Three elements are required to establish disparate impact. Firstly, a facially-neutral employment practice, secondly a disproportionately-adverse impact on a protected group, and thirdly, a causal-nexus between the practice and the adverse impact. Once disparate impact is made out the business necessity defence can provide employer-defendants the opportunity to argue that the discriminatory practice is essential to the continued viability of their business.[372] During the 1970's following *Griggs*, disparate impact became an

---

368 Justin Cummins and Beth Isle, 'Towards Systemic Equality. Reinvigorating a Progressive Application of the Disparate Impact Doctrine' *Mitchell Hamline Law Review* 43(1), 102–139: 106.

369 *Griggs v. Duke Powers*, 401 U.S. 424 (1971).

370 *Ibid.*, at para 431.

371 Rosemary Hunter and Elaine Shoben, 'Disparate Impact Discrimination: American Oddity or Internationally Accepted Concept?' *Berkeley Journal of Employment and Labour Law* 19(108) (1998), 108–152: 113.

372 Susan S. Grover, 'The Business Necessity Defense in Disparate Impact Discrimination Cases' *College of William and Mary Law School* (1996) William & Mary Law School Scholarship Repository.

important tool for addressing covert discrimination.[373] In addition, the courts set out a burden-shifting framework specifying who bears the burden of proof in the business necessity defence. Once a plaintiff has made out the elements of disparate impact, the defendant has the initial burden of proof to establish a business justification. After that the burden shifts back to the plaintiff who has an opportunity to show that the business justification is a 'pretext' for sex discrimination. The plaintiff can demonstrate an alternative method of achieving business aims without discrimination as a way of illustrating that pretext.[374]

In the 1977 successful disparate impact case of *Dothard v. Rawlinson,*[375] the plaintiff applied to be a prison guard but was rejected because she failed to meet the minimum 120-pound weight requirement of the Alabama statute that set out the requirements for prison guards. The law also had a height minimum of 5 feet 2 inches.[376] The plaintiff produced national statistics as to the comparative height and weight of men and women, indicating that Alabama's statutory standards would exclude over 4 percent of the female population but less than 1 percent of the male population.[377] The court agreed that this established disparate impact because the facially neutral standards result in a significantly discriminatory pattern. The employer could not make out a business justification defence because there was no evidence that the height and weight standards were necessary for effective job performance.[378]

Despite early successes in discrimination claims during the 1980's, the composition of the Supreme Court became more conservative and the disparate impact doctrine began to weaken.[379] In two cases at the end of the 1980's, two shifts made disparate impact claims more difficult.[380] Firstly, the courts determined the plaintiff must identify a specific employment practice that causes the disparate impact, and secondly, instead of a burden of persuasion on the defendant in relation to business necessity, the burden was lightened to one of production (which may or may not be convincing), before shifting back to

373 Robert Belton, 'The Crusade for Equality in the Workplace. The Griggs v. Duke Power Story' (University Press of Kansas, 2014).

374 *Albemarle Paper Co v. Moody*, 422 U.S. 405 (1975).

375 *Dothard* above n. 358.

376 *Dothard* above n. 358, at para 24.

377 *Dothard* above n. 358, at para 25.

378 *Dothard* above n. 358, at para 26.

379 Cummins and Isle above n. 368, 111; and Linda Cheng Yee Lye 'Title VII's Tangled Tale: The Erosion and Confusion of Disparate Impact and the Business Necessity Defense' *Berkeley Journal of Employment and Labor Law* 19(2) (1998), 315–336.

380 Cummins and Isle, above n. 368, 120.

the plaintiff to establish there is a non-discriminatory alternative to the defendant's legitimate business goals.[381]

Subsequently, Congress amended Title VII in 1991 to expressly include disparate impact claims. The amendment made clear that the plaintiff must identify a specific employment practice creating the disparate impact, although with an exception if it is not possible to separate the defendant's actions into a single practice, codifying the Supreme Court's decision in *Wards Cove*.[382] Secondly, it specifically defined business necessity as 'job related for the position in question and consistent with business necessity.' Thirdly, it raised the standard of proof requiring persuasion (and not merely production).[383] Fourthly, it changed the requirement that the plaintiff establish a 'non-discriminatory alternative' to an 'equally effective' alternative, a much higher burden. Fifthly and significantly, successful disparate impact claims were entitled to only equitable remedies.[384]

These changes did not lead to an expansion of disparate impact claims, rather they led to their retraction. This can likely be attributed to some of the amendments, which restricted claims, combined with the appointment of a series of conservative Supreme Court judges by the Reagan administration.[385] Examples of the barriers in the requirements of disparate impact since the 1991 amendments include the following. Firstly, the requirement to identify a specific employment practice which caused the disparate impact has proven difficult in many cases. For example, in the 1997 case of *Clark v. Eagle Food Centres*,[386] the plaintiff was employed as an Assistant Store Manager, but was not promoted to a Store Manager position, instead younger males, with shorter service were promoted. She successfully produced statistical evidence showing a clear disparate impact on women in terms of promotion and hiring, however she did not identify a specific practice that was the cause of that outcome. The Eighth Circuit held the failure to identify a specific employment practice doomed her action.[387]

Secondly, as in disparate treatment cases, causation is a difficult hurdle in disparate impact cases. For example, in the 2000 case of *EEOC v. Joe's Stone*

381 *Wards Cove Packing Company v. Antonio*, 490 U.S. 642 (1989).

382 *Civil Rights Act* 1964, 42 U.S.C. 2000e-2(k)(1)(A)(i).

383 Hunter and Shoben, above n. 371, 113.

384 Melissa Hart, 'From Wards Cove to Ricci. Struggling Against the 'Built in Headwinds' of a Skeptical Court' *Wake Forest Law Review* 46 (2011), 261–279.

385 *Ibid.*

386 *Clark v. Eagle Food Centres*, 105 F.3d 662 (8th Cir).

387 *Ibid.*, at para 6.

Crab Inc.,[388] a seafood restaurant in Miami Beach employed 108 food servers between 1991 and 1995, all of whom were male.[389] The female plaintiffs argued disparate impact, because, despite no specific rule that women could not be employed, there were no women servers.[390] Causation was problematic because only 3 percent of applicants were female. However, the reason the number of female applicants was so low was because it was well-known that the defendant employed men servers to maintain an 'Old World' ambience of 'fine dining' in which 'tuxedo clad men served its distinctive menus.'[391] This made it difficult, however, for the plaintiffs to establish a causative link between a specific employment practice and the sex disparity. Hiring decisions were made by the daytime maître d, according to the defendant, based on 'appearance, articulation, attitude and experience.'[392] The defendant owner stated: 'I cannot explain the predominance of male servers but perhaps it has to do with the very heavy trays to be carried, the ambience of the restaurant and the extremely low turnover in servers.'[393] Ultimately, the Eleventh Circuit held there was no causative link between any specific employment practice and the gender disparity.[394] Rather the reputation of the defendant's discriminatory hiring practices was the cause because it deterred women from applying.[395] This extraordinary reasoning found that reputation is not a practice nor a specific act. The court stated: 'Reputation is a prevalent or common belief, a general name, the opinion of a number of persons.'[396] The court did not see the hiring practices as a facially-neutral systematic exclusion that over time caused qualified female applicants to self-select themselves out of the hiring process.[397]

Finally, because the 1991 amendments allowed for only equitable remedies rather than the compensatory and punitive damages available for claims of intentional disparate treatment cases, many plaintiffs may have elected to pursue disparate treatment claims rather than disparate impact.[398]

388 *EEOC v. Joe's Stone Crab Inc.*, 220 F.3d 1263 (11th Cir.2000).
389 *Ibid.*, at para 5.
390 *Ibid.*, at para 32.
391 *Ibid.*, at para 48.
392 *Ibid.*, at para 7.
393 *Ibid.*, at para 11.
394 *Ibid.*, at para 44, 45.
395 *Ibid.*, at para 45.
396 *Ibid.*, at para 44.
397 *Ibid.*, at para 49, 51.
398 Barry, above n. 357, 179.

3.2 *The Application of Sex Protection in Australia*

Australia, established in 1901 as a federation of six states and two territories through the *Constitution of Australia* 1901 (Constitution), is a party to the *ICCPR*, *IESCR* and *CEDAW*. There are multiple established avenues for pursuing sex discrimination claims despite the absence of a Bill of Rights in the Australian Constitution. The first avenues were state-based legislation, including South Australia in 1966[399] and New South Wales and Victoria in 1977,[400] primarily focused on workplace exclusion. Australia subsequently acceded to *CEDAW* on 28 July 1983 and the *Sex Discrimination Act* 1984 (Cth) (SDA) and the focus of this section was enacted the following year utilizing the external affairs power of the Constitution.[401] The 1984 SDA, a federal law applying to all of Australia, was the first comprehensive national anti-discrimination legislation enacted in Australia and provides the most substantial avenue of redress for victims of sex discrimination. Other laws with sex discrimination provisions followed, including the *Industrial Relations Act* 1988 (Cth), *Fair Work Act* 2009 (Cth). Sex discrimination legislation has now been enacted in each state and territory.[402]

The SDA proscribes discrimination on multiple grounds including sex, which is defined to include a characteristic that appertains 'generally' or is 'generally imputed' to 'persons of the sex of the aggrieved person' implicitly incorporating gender into the meaning of sex.[403] The ambit of operation is restricted to areas of public or quasi-public life, including employment, education, goods and services, accommodation, land and clubs.[404] Discrimination can be direct or indirect, neither of which requires intent although indirect discrimination is lawful if the circumstances are 'reasonable'.[405] Direct discrimination requires a comparator treated more favourably and must be 'by reason' of sex.[406]

Indirect discrimination, in the original enactment of SDA, was when a person requires another to comply with a requirement or condition 'with which a substantially higher proportion of persons of the opposite sex to the aggrieved person comply or are able to comply which is not reasonable having regard to

399 *Prohibition of Discrimination Act* 1966 (SA).

400 *Anti-Discrimination Act* 1977 (NSW); and *Equal Opportunity Act* 1977 (Vic).

401 *Constitution of Australia* 1901, s. 51.

402 *Equal Opportunity Act* 1984 (SA); *Anti-Discrimination Act* 1977 (NSW); *Equal Opportunity Act* 1995 (Vic); *Equal Opportunity Act* 1984 (WA); *Anti-Discrimination Act* 1991 (Qld); *Discrimination Act* 1991 (ACT); *Anti-Discrimination Act* 1992 (NT); and *Sex Discrimination Act* 1994 (Tas).

403 SDA, s. 5(1).

404 SDA, Part II.

405 SDA, s. 5.

406 SDA, s. 5(1).

the circumstances of the case; and with which the aggrieved person does not or is not able to comply.' The text was amended in 1995 after a parliamentary review with the intent of making indirect discrimination more accessible. The ability of a 'substantially higher proportion of persons of the opposite sex' to comply was replaced with a condition, requirement or practice 'that has, or is likely to have, the effect of disadvantaging persons of the same sex as the aggrieved person.'[407] The amendments to the SDA also shifted the burden of establishing reasonableness from the plaintiff to the defendant, making it a defence, and set out the meaning of reasonableness more fully, although without altering the meaning of reasonableness itself.[408] There has been a significant flow of direct discrimination cases since the SDA was enacted in 1984, but a much smaller volume of indirect discrimination cases even after the amendments in 1995. The next two subsections consider how the Australian Human Rights Commission (AHRC) and the courts have interpreted the SDA in relation to sex discrimination based on the two forms of discrimination – direct discrimination and indirect discrimination.[409]

3.2.1 Direct Discrimination

Direct sex discrimination under the SDA occurs when a person by reason of sex or a characteristic that appertains generally to persons of the sex of the aggrieved person, or a characteristic that is generally imputed to persons of the sex of the aggrieved person, 'treats the aggrieved person less favourably than, in circumstances that are the same or are not materially different, the discriminator treats or would treat a person of a different sex.'[410] The two elements to establish direct discrimination are clearly embedded in the text of the legislation. The first element is a requirement for comparison with a person of a 'different sex' who is or would be treated more favourably in circumstances that are the same or are not materially different. The second element is causation, expressed in the legislation by the words 'by reason of' requiring a causal connection between the less favourable treatment and sex. Evidence of the reasons for the discriminatory decision or conduct, so that sex can be established as a cause are required although as the cases below indicate there is a lack of consistency on this element. Intention or motive need not be proven, in accord with the approach taken by the *CEDAW* Committee, the HRC and the

407 SDA, s. 5(2).

408 SDA, s. 7B.

409 The Australian Human Rights Commission hears complaints of sex discrimination under the SDA as first instance. A decision of the Commission can be appealed to the Federal Court.

410 SDA, s. 5(1).

CESCR. The following subsections consider examples of the application of the two main elements for establishing direct sex discrimination – an opposite-sex comparator and causation. A range of case examples is then reviewed in discrete areas where sex discrimination claims have been pursued.

3.2.1.1 *Opposite-Sex Comparator*

The requirement for a comparator of a person of a different sex treated more favourably is explicit in the SDA. In straightforward cases, the requirement does not prevent a finding of direct sex discrimination, however, in more nuanced and complex cases, where an opposite-sex comparator is not so easily identified, this has resulted in unfavourable findings. For example, in a straightforward and successful case in 1994 *Djokic v. Sinclair & Central Qld Meat Export Co Pty Ltd.*,[411] the plaintiff successfully claimed direct discrimination in relation to her employment in a meatworks. She applied to be trained as a slicer but was denied the opportunity because it was considered 'men's work'.[412] Instead, women should pack, which is women's work, and paid less than a slicer. The judge found the plaintiff could perform the duties of a slicer and a straightforward comparison with male slicers led to a finding of direct sex discrimination.[413]

In *Ho v. Regulator Australia Pty Ltd and Anor* in 2004,[414] although less straightforward than *Djokic v. Sinclair*, the plaintiff successfully argued direct sex discrimination. The plaintiff worked for a small business and argued that after revealing her pregnancy to the defendant she was required to undertake the demeaning task of changing towels in the men's washroom.[415] The judge found the request to change the towels was not made because the plaintiff was pregnant. Instead, it was made 'because the job needed doing and it was a job that had always been done by one of the girls.'[416] The request would not have been made if the plaintiff had been a man. It follows, the court held, that requesting the plaintiff to change the towels in the men's washroom, meant she was treated less favourably than a man would have been treated in the same circumstances.[417] In this case the judge had no difficulty in understanding the gendered nature of the request to find direct sex discrimination.

---

411 *Djokic v. Sinclair & Central Qld Meat Export Co Pty Ltd* [1994] HREOCA 16 (24 August 1994).
412 *Ibid.*
413 *Ibid.*
414 *Ho v. Regulator* Australia *Pty Ltd & Anor* [2004] FMCA 62 (12 May 2004).
415 *Ibid.*, at para 18.
416 *Ibid.*, at para 151.
417 *Ibid.*, at para 151.

In a more complex case in 2005, *Zhang v. Kanellos & Anor*,[418] the plaintiff argued that the defendant ordered her to wear a mini-skirt in the hotel gaming room where she worked as an attendant and this constituted direct sex discrimination. She argued that she was treated less favourably than a male employee would have been in the same or similar circumstances.[419] The defendant argued the only comparator available is another female, and although that female was not required to wear a mini-skirt, he had an agreement with the plaintiff that she wear a mini-skirt.[420] Although the plaintiff claimed the defendant stated to her: 'There's gonna be new rules for you, Susie, if you don't wear a mini-skirt next time I will grab your boobs,'[421] the judge held there was no opposite-sex comparator available. 'They are both women. There were no other employees in the gaming area at the hotel against whom Ms Zhang's treatment might be compared' he stated, 'Even on the basis of a hypothetical comparison, there is no evidence that a male employee, if there had been one in the gaming room, would have been treated any differently.'[422] The obligation on the plaintiff to wear mini-skirts came from a consensual agreement and the judge stated 'she admitted owning short skirts and wearing them socially.'[423] This astonishing conclusion, given the unlikelihood of a male employee being asked to dress in a way that is clearly intended as sexually alluring to the male clients in the gaming room, illustrates the vast differences in how judges can and do approach their analysis of a real or hypothetical comparator. While the judge in *Ho* easily recognized the gendered nature of a request to change towels in the bathroom, this judge was unable to recognize the gendered nature of a request to wear a mini-skirt in a gaming room.

In the 2013 case of *Margan v. President, Australian Human Rights Commission*,[424] the plaintiffs argued that their inability to register same-sex marriages in the states of New South Wales, Queensland, Victoria, South Australia and the Australian Capital Territory was direct sex discrimination.[425] The court dismissed the argument on the basis of formal (in) equality. The court reasoned that a man cannot enter into marriage with another man and a woman cannot enter into a marriage with another woman and therefore both men and women are being treated in the same way and there is no sex

418 *Zhang v. Kanellos & Anor* [2005] FMCA 111 (11 March 2005).
419 *Ibid.*, at para 4.
420 *Ibid.*, at para 59.
421 *Ibid.*, at para 50.
422 *Ibid.*, at para 60.
423 *Ibid.*, at para 61.
424 *Margan v. President, Australian Human Rights Commission* [2013] FCA 109.
425 *Ibid.*, at para 2.

discrimination.[426] A different reasoning, however, would be to, instead of comparing women who cannot marry women with men who cannot marry men, compare a woman who cannot marry another woman with a man who can marry that same woman. This different reasoning clearly indicates that this is a difference based on sex.

In the 2018 case of *Barnett v. Royal Queensland Golf Club*,[427] the plaintiff, an avid golfer, successfully argued direct discrimination under the SDA by the golf club to which she belonged as a full member. The plaintiff's membership stipulated that she was entitled to access the golf course and play 18 holes of golf each day of the week. However, the club scheduled a regular 18-hole competition on Wednesdays in which only male members were eligible to participate, which had tee off times from 6:30 a.m. to 8:15 a.m. and from 11:00 a.m. to 12:45 p.m. This meant that female members could not be on the course from 6:30 a.m. until 3:00 p.m. and, depending on the time of year, could not complete 18 holes of golf in one session. Although there were female only slots on other days the timings did not reasonably prevent male golfers from completing an 18-hole round.[428] The court began its examination of direct discrimination by identifying the need for an opposite-sex comparator, which it named as a male full member of the Golf Club. A male full member who wished to play 18 holes of golf may do so on any day of the week, even on days when there was a female-only competition being played, because the timing did not prevent them from doing so.[429] The court concluded that restricting female members from enjoying a benefit of membership of the Golf Club that is otherwise available to male members of the same membership category is to treat the former less favourably than the latter. The plaintiff was treated therefore less favourably because of her sex.[430] Like the early case of *Djokic* where women were denied the opportunity to be slicers, this case is successful because there is an easily identifiable male comparator, treated more favourably.

By contrast, in the 2019 case of *Coady v. Yachting Victoria Inc.*,[431] the female plaintiff was unsuccessful. The plaintiff entered a 'male only' competition at the Sailing World Cup Melbourne regatta with her father as crew. She knew that a mixed-sex Olympic class was also available that she and her father could have entered, however, she said that to compete in that race, they needed to

426 *Ibid.*, at para 23, 24.
427 *Barnett v. Royal Queensland Golf Club* [2018] FCCA 3697 (12 December 2018).
428 *Ibid.*, at para 23.
429 *Ibid.*, at para 25.
430 *Ibid.*, at para 34.
431 *Coady v. Yachting Victoria Inc.* [2019] FCCA 2095 (2 August 2019).

sail a 'Nacra' (boat) and we didn't have a Nacra boat, so it was not an option.'[432] She further stated that while there was a female-only open race she could have competed in, her boat would have placed her at a disadvantage over everyone else so she decided not to sail in that event. The plaintiff further said: 'It's very, very difficult to find a female that is suited to me. I'm not big and strong. I need a very, very strong crew to help me in the female rig if I wanted to sail in – with a FX rig that would have been also another option but finding a female crew is very difficult.'[433] She sailed in the male-only event but was disqualified and subsequently lodged a claim of direct sex discrimination. The court held there was no direct sex discrimination. The comparator, they said 'would be a man who had, notwithstanding the clear rules of race specifying the Olympic gender requirements, sought to enter and compete in the female Olympic class event, namely the 49FX.'[434] The court held that in those circumstances, the male comparator would be similarly disqualified and therefore there was no less favourable treatment in the same or similar circumstances.[435] This reasoning illustrates again the weakness of an opposite-sex comparator approach. The plaintiff was clearly 'excluded' from the race in which she wanted to enter with no obvious similar alternative for her. She is not advantaged in the competition and the comparison to a male who likely would be advantaged does not equate to circumstances that are the same or are not materially different.

3.2.1.2 *'By Reason of' Sex: Causation*

The second element to establishing direct sex discrimination is causation, expressed in the legislation the words 'by reason of'. Although sex must be one of the causes of the discrimination, it need not be the only reason for the discrimination. Despite this, causation has proven to be a stumbling block in many cases to come before the courts where the courts have not recognized a link between the unfavourable treatment and sex, often relying on gender stereotypes in their reasoning.[436]

For example, in the 1985 case of *Fenwick v. Beveridge Building Products*[437] shortly after the enactment of the SDA, the plaintiff was employed at Beveridge Building Products, which sells hardware products, as a sales assistant. The plaintiff, who worked a 30-hour week, was given notice of employment

432 *Ibid.*, at para 72.

433 *Ibid.*, at para 74.

434 *Ibid.*, at para 169.

435 *Ibid.*, at para 170.

436 *Shaw v. Perpetual Trustees* [1993] HREOCA 19 (10 September 1993); and *Van Druten v. Sheraton Pacific Hotels Pty Ltd* [1996] HREOCA 23 (29 July 1996).

437 *Fenwick v. Beveridge Building Products Pty Ltd* [1985] HREOCA 1 (2 October 1985).

termination on the basis that they needed a full-time person. She argued she was not asked to increase her hours, and her dismissal was direct sex discrimination. She argued that she experienced sex discrimination during her approximately one-year employment which led to her dismissal. This included her employer insisting upon her remaining in the open shed where the sales area was situated, even in the depth of winter when it was very cold, while allowing the men to remain indoors in the warmth. The defendant allowed the men to have breaks but refused to allow her and her colleague, who had been good friends for a long period, to have morning tea together. The defendant agreed he treated her less favourably but claimed it was not because of sex but because of her 'tendency to chatter during work hours'.[438] While agreeing that the men were given preference, the court stated: 'We also believe, from all the evidence, that the complainant did like to gossip with members of the staff.' The court went on to state of the defendant: 'It is probable that he did not like women who were dominant or self-assertive.'[439] It was her tendency to gossip, that she was dominant and self-assertive and because the employer 'was uncomfortable in working with women who were employed in occupations which he did not regard being traditionally those of women' that caused the unfavourable treatment. This astonishing reasoning does not connect the defendant's characterization of the plaintiff as having a 'tendency to gossip' to be 'dominant and self-assertive' and his statement that he did not like such women and that he 'was uncomfortable in working with women who were employed in occupations which he did not regard being traditionally those of women' with gender. This case illustrates an inability of some male judges to recognize linkages between gendered stereotypes and less favourable treatment of women who display 'unacceptable' behaviour for women workers.

In the 1992 case of *Re Mount Isa Mines Limited v. Lou Marks*,[440] multiple plaintiffs argued that a proposed national code of practice for the control and safe use of inorganic lead at work that differentiated between men and women was sex discrimination. The Tribunal held that it was sex discrimination.[441] On appeal however the federal court disagreed and held that the discrimination was based on health, not sex.[442] Causation therefore was not established.

438 *Ibid.*

439 *Ibid.*

440 *Re Mount Isa Mines Limited v. Lou Marks; Edward Emmett; Jennifer George; Clive Brown; Jennifer Massie; David Nolan; Robert Hart; Kerry Klineberg; Barry Nutter; Neil Bartholomaeus; Leslie Wright; Darcy Mcgaurr; John Thomson; Sarah Butterworth; Barry Durh* [1992] FCA 104 (13 March 1992).

441 *Ibid.*, at para 5.

442 *Ibid.*, at para 14.

Causation was not established in the 1995 case of *Gilroy v. Curley* as the judge did not perceive any linkage between the defendant's conduct and the plaintiff's sex. The plaintiff was employed as a security guard and wore the defendant's uniform. She was dismissed and subsequently claimed direct sex discrimination. A witness stated that the defendant did not like the plaintiff wearing their uniform because she did not fit the company image because she was a 'small female' with 'bits missing' and 'no nuts'.[443] The defendant also stated he needed 'big blokes, six feet high' working for him. The judge however did not believe the witness, nor the plaintiff and he stated that even if the defendant did make the statements, they were not related to her gender. Instead, the judge held the dismissal was related to the collapse of the relationship between the two partners that employed her.[444]

Similar reasoning, where the judge was unable to see the connection between a defendant's conduct and sex, was applied in the 2018 case of *Von Schoeler v. Alan Taylor*.[445] The plaintiff was employed in a plywood factory as a grader and claimed that she had been sexually harassed over many years at her workplace. It began when a fellow employee 'approached her from behind and touched her on the area of her buttocks.' She reported this to her supervisor but was unsatisfied with the response and eventually made a formal complaint. After she made the complaint, she was subject to abuse including being calling a 'slut' and a 'dobbing dog'.[446] There was a series of other incidents and a year later the plaintiff was moved onto night shifts, which she characterized as a demotion. The judge held that '[i]t cannot be established …that any treatment occurred because the applicant was a woman.'[447]

3.2.1.3 *Sexual Harassment*

Plaintiffs in numerous cases have argued that they have been sexually harassed in the workplace, creating difficulties in maintaining their jobs and sometimes resulting in their dismissal as their ability to perform their job diminished. Although the cases uniformly accept sexual harassment as a form of sex discrimination, there is inconsistency as to whether the judge believes the plaintiffs or recognizes the experiences of the plaintiffs as sexual harassment. Indeed, there are far fewer cases where the judge believes the plaintiff, than those where the judge disbelieves the plaintiff.

---

443 *Ibid.*, at para 15.

444 *Gilroy v. Curley* [1995] HREOCA 1 (12 January 1995).

445 *Von Schoeler v. Alan Taylor & Company Ltd Trading as Boral Timber & Ors* [2018] FCCA 3932.

446 *Ibid.*, at para 13, 15.

447 *Ibid.*, at para 39.

Judges in the following cases recognized sexual harassment and found direct sex discrimination as a result. In the 1991 case of *A v. Caboolture Shire Council*,[448] the plaintiff claimed she was dismissed after a period of sexual harassment led to her missing work. The defendant claimed she was dismissed because the number of days she had been absent from work and because of complaints from the other members of the gang in which she worked that she could not or would not do 'heavy' work, such as picking up (big) rocks and pushing wheelbarrows.[449] The court agreed that the work absenteeism was related to sexual harassment and that sex discrimination 'must include as discrimination, that species involving sexual harassment.'[450] *In Zoiti v. Cheesecake Factory & Quirk*, the plaintiff was told she was a sweetie and 'better looking' than the last girl and had 'big tits'.[451] In *San v. Dirluck Pty Ltd & Anor*, the plaintiff was told she must endear herself to 'those who pay you'.[452] In *Harwin v. Pateluch,* the judge did not accept that 'ruffling of a young female employee's hair by an older supervisor as amounting to conduct of a "sexual nature" inappropriate as it may be.' He did, however, accept that 'frequent touching on the bottom' was.[453] In *Frith v. The Exchange Hotel & Anor*, the judge said the plaintiff was 'generally a truthful witness and like many women in the workplace (who are usually the unfortunate victims of this type of activity) she was 'reluctant to make her feelings known.'[454] In *Rankilor v. Jerome Pty Ltd*,[455] the plaintiff claimed she was verbally abused in public in a store when pursuing a complaint about a defective sofa bed, and that some of the insulting language denigrated her on the basis of her gender. She claimed the defendant said: 'you stupid woman' and 'you useless woman' and 'you're only a woman.'[456] The judge believed her. The real issue, the judge stated, was whether the degree and content of the abuse was caused by her gender, so as to be able to conclude that she was 'treated less favourably' than a man. He concluded that causation was established because to reference gender in derogatory and insulting terms revealed an attitude in relation to a female customer which was unlikely to have influenced his reaction to a male customer.[457] In *Employment Services*

448 *A v. Caboolture Shire Council* [1991] HREOCA 11 (15 November 1991).
449 *Ibid.*
450 *Ibid.*
451 *Zoiti v. Cheesecake Factory & Quirk* [1993] HREOCA 12.
452 *San v. Dirluck Pty Ltd & Anor* [2005] FMCA 750 (9 June 2005).
453 *Harwin v. Pateluch* [1995] HREOCA 23 (21 August 1995).
454 *Frith v. The Exchange Hotel &* Anor [2005] FMCA 402 (1 April 2005) e32.
455 *Rankilor v. Jerome Pty Ltd* [2006] FMCA 922 (30 June 2006).
456 *Ibid.*, at para 15.
457 *Ibid.*, at para 28.

Australia Pty Ltd v. Poniatowska,[458] the judge concluded that the plaintiff was dismissed 'because she was a female who would not tolerate sexual harassment and the robust work environment.'[459] The defendant, the judge held, considered her complaints about the way she was treated in the workplace and her refusal to accept the sexual harassment to which she was subjected as an impediment to the smooth running of his business. The judge at first instance, and the judge on appeal, both held that the defendant 'would not have taken the same approach to a male who was sexually harassed and had complained. That is, he would not have considered that male to be an impediment to the smooth running of the business. It was all of those factors that resulted in the termination of her employment.'[460] In all these cases the judges believed the plaintiffs and found sex discrimination.

There are however a significant number of cases where the judges did not believe the plaintiffs' version of events.[461] Analyzing these cases without the benefit of the evidence presented to the judge is difficult, however, it is notable that there are many examples of judges preferring the testimony of defendants. Additionally, there is an extensive body of research and literature that documents the tendency of the courts and other gatekeepers to disbelieve women's versions of sexual harassment.[462] Disbelief is often based on negative cultural stereotypes about women's motives for seeking redress for harms; and on deep-rooted cultural belief that women as a group are inherently less than fully trustworthy.[463]

In the 2006 case of *Wiggins v. Department of Defence – Navy*,[464] involving a claim of sexual harassment in the navy, the judge believed the officer against whom the complaints were made; 'who I find was a witness of truth' and 'in the absence of specific reliable corroboration, I do not accept the substantive allegations of sex discrimination claimed to constitute discrimination pursuant to the provisions of the SDA have been established.'[465]

458 *Employment Services Australia Pty Ltd v. Poniatowska* [2010] FCAFC 92.

459 *Ibid.*

460 *Ibid.*, at para 114.

461 *Liddle v. Morley* [1994] HREOCA 7 (23 March 1994) not proven; and *Holmyard v. Jones t/a Wynyard Cleaning Service* [1995] HREOCA 11 (15 March 1995)

462 Deborah Epstein, 'Discounting Credibility: Doubting the Stories of Women Survivors of Sexual Harassment' *Available*, at *SSRN 3575843* (2020).

463 Patricia Recupero, The Notion of Truth and Our Evolving Understanding of Sexual Harassment' *Journal of the American Academy of Psychiatry and the Law* 46(1) (2018), 23–30.

464 Leigh Gilmore, *Tainted Witness: Why we Doubt what Women say about their Lives* (Columbia University Press, 2017).

465 *Wiggins v. Department of Defence – Navy* [2006] FMCA 800 (9 June 2006), at para 120.

The judge in the 2010 case of *Taric v. Ahmed & Anor* did not believe the plaintiff's account of the sexual harassment she experienced.[466] The plaintiff was employed in the office of the defendant's business, which involves the design, fabrication and installation of balustrading. The plaintiff argued she was dismissed after a period of sexual harassment which included, she claimed, statements from her employer that 'he had wanted to hire a particular Lebanese woman but she was so beautiful that someone, whom the applicant inferred was him, could lose control' and that 'extra-marital sex was customary amongst all Australian married couples.' Although noting that it is sufficient if the relevant discriminatory characteristic, namely her sex, was 'a reason' for the alleged conduct, and it need not have been the real reason' or the 'only reason,' for the conduct, and despite the defendant describing her work as 'very good, indeed flawless' the judge found the plaintiff's evidence 'contrived and implausible'[467] and that she was an unconvincing and unimpressive witness.[468] It is puzzling the judge could accept that a worker could perform effectively in her duties yet be 'contrived, unconvincing and unimpressive' in her testimony.

The plaintiff in the 2014 case of *Romero v. Farstad Shipping (Indian Pacific) Pty Ltd*[469] was employed as a maritime officer aboard the defendant's supply vessels, which transported material to oil and gas platforms in Bass Strait. She claimed that she had been harassed by her employer. The behaviour included ignoring her chain of command, leading other crew members into thinking she had mismanaged ship equipment, calling her incompetent, ignoring her professional assessment of safety equipment, and telling her she had a mental health problem.[470] The judge did not find this conduct connected to the plaintiff's gender. Indeed, Captain Martin claimed he would have behaved in the same way towards male crew members, although there was no evidence he did so. The judge stated: 'I found Captain Martin to be a credible witness. The poor relationship between Captain Martin and Ms Romero was the result of an escalating personality clash rather than any sex discrimination on Captain Martin's part.'[471] The judge went on to state: 'I do not find Captain Martin's observation of Ms Romero as "an older female under stress", if this is indeed what he said, to be anything more than a factual statement; she was indeed a female, and based on her own evidence in chief, was under considerable stress

466 *Taric v. Ahmed & Anor* [2010] FMCA 479 (14 July 2010).
467 *Ibid.*, at para 70.
468 *Ibid.*, at para 75.
469 *Romero v. Farstad Shipping (Indian Pacific) Pty Ltd* [2014] FCA 439.
470 *Ibid.*, at para 12.
471 *Ibid.*, at para 17.

while on the Far Swan.'[472] The accepted conduct of the defendant, particularly given the plaintiff was working in a male dominated industry, appears very connected to her sex, despite the conclusions of the judge.

Finally, the judges in two 2015 cases did not believe the plaintiffs' accounts of sexual harassment. In the first, *TN v. BF & Anor*,[473] the plaintiff, a Vietnamese woman in her mid-twenties for whom English was a second language, was employed as a salesperson by the defendant, the business that employed her, and the second defendant, the founder of the company who still attended the workplace, although he played no active role in running the company (AB).[474] The plaintiff was interviewed for the job by AB and, according to her, he asked her to raise her skirt and masturbate, which she refused to do. He then started masturbating. AB claimed, in contrast, that he had commented critically on the plaintiff's skirt length, saying that she needed to wear more appropriate attire, and that, in response, she had said 'how about this?' and lifted up her skirt and started masturbating.[475] AB stated that he masturbated in response. In a separate incident, a few days later, AB admitted to masturbating in the presence of both the plaintiff and another staff member. The plaintiff videoed AB on her phone without his knowledge, while he masturbated for four and a half minutes. Astonishingly the judge believed AB, despite the video and the testimony of the other staff member. He put great reliance on the plaintiff's personality disorder finding that the plaintiff had a 'propensity to exaggerate and embellish events'.[476]

3.2.1.4 *Maternity Leave Return*

In a series of cases, women have returned from maternity or parental leave to find their position gone or reduced in responsibilities, and they have argued direct sex discrimination. These have been difficult cases to win as illustrated below, in part because the opposite-sex comparators utilized by the courts do not provide a real equivalence.[477] Since only women can take maternity leave, and it is predominantly women who take parental leave, it is therefore a form of leave for which there can be no reasonable male comparator.

---

472 *Ibid.*, at para 20.

473 *TN v. BF & Anor* [2015] FCCA 1497 (12 June 2015).

474 *Ibid.*, at para 2.

475 *Ibid.*, at para 104.

476 *Ibid.*, at para 88; and see Karen O'Connell, 'Can Law Address Intersectional Sexual Harassment? The Case of Claimants with Personality Disorders' *Laws, MDPI*, Open Access Journal 8(4) (2019), 1–14: 7.

477 *TN v. BF Ibid.*, at para 77.

In 1998, a plaintiff who argued both direct and indirect sex discrimination relating to a series of adverse events at her place of employment, was successful on a number of indirect sex discrimination actions, however unsuccessful at establishing direct discrimination.[478] The plaintiff commenced as a lawyer with the defendant in 1988 at age 24. She began working in the insurance group and later moved to plaintiff-practice. She progressed rapidly and was promoted to the position of Associate in 1991. In 1994, she expanded her insurance work while continuing the plaintiff work and in 1995 she became a contract partner appointed for a term of one year. At the time of this appointment, the plaintiff was pregnant, a fact known to the firm, and she commenced maternity leave before the expiry of the one-year term. During her maternity leave her plaintiff work was transferred to another lawyer and when she returned to work part-time in 1996 her practice had been reduced to insurance work. The defendant decided not to renew her contract when it terminated, and she left the firm.[479]

The plaintiff made multiple claims of direct sex discrimination due to the failure of the defendant to make proper provision to support her practice during her maternity leave and when she returned to part-time work.[480] She argued that if a male partner had taken leave, a solicitor would have been put in charge of the practice or other steps taken to maintain it for the partner. The court stated: 'The difficulty is to define the male person with whom she should be compared, for the purposes of s. 5(1).' Comparing the plaintiff 'with a male partner who was absent for some weeks and whose legal staff had left, for whatever reason, it might be reasonable to infer that temporary arrangements would be made to maintain that partner's practice and that reasonable steps would be taken to that end, such as assigning a solicitor from inside the firm or from outside.'[481] The court, however, viewed the plaintiff's position as more complicated because of her intent to return to part-time, rather than full-time, work.[482] 'The workload in her practice appears to have been more than could be maintained by one person working part-time. This appears to have been a factor in the decision.' While the judge agreed that that maternity leave is connected with being a woman (and therefore sex discrimination), the judge did not agree that that any of the alleged acts of discrimination were committed 'by reason of' the plaintiff's maternity leave (or sex). Causation therefore was not made out despite suspecting that 'the firm might have made some

478 *Hickie v. Hunt & Hunt* [1998] HREOCA 8 (9 March 1998).
479 *Ibid.*, at para 1.7.
480 *Ibid.*, at para 1.8.
481 *Ibid.*, at para 4.5.20.
482 *Ibid.*, at para 4.5.20.

efforts to maintain the practice of a male partner until his return, even if, in the long run, it was their policy to wind down the plaintiff-practice.'[483]

In the 2002 case of *Thomson v. Orica*,[484] the plaintiff successfully argued her employer directly discriminated against her on the ground of sex (amongst other things). The plaintiff had worked for the defendant for 10 years as accounts manager, and upon becoming pregnant, informed her employer she planned to take a twelve-months maternity leave. According to the plaintiff, the defendant shouted over the telephone and said that he 'would never employ a female again' and that 'there's laws against this' and that 'now I've got three women on maternity leave.'[485] This tirade reduced her to tears. She did, however, take maternity leave but when she returned to work, she was given different duties and responsibilities to those performed prior to her maternity leave, of significantly reduced status and responsibility, although on the same pay. The court reasoned that the plaintiff was treated less favourably than an equivalent person who was not pregnant by giving her tasks, duties and responsibilities of significantly reduced status on her return.[486] The demotion in status, they held, would have affected detrimentally her access to opportunities for promotion.

The plaintiff in *Sheaves v. AAPT Limited*[487] had been employed from 1998 to 2004 as one of three accounts manager when she went on maternity leave. Another accounts manager was employed to replace her during her absence but by the time she returned to work there were only two accounts managers.[488] After her return, the defendant decided that he needed only two accounts managers and the plaintiff was terminated a few weeks later.[489] The court utilized as a comparator an accounts manager who was not pregnant who took twelve months of leave and had a right to return to the former position. The court found that such a person would have been treated the same as the plaintiff, since the defendant ultimately needed only two accounts managers. The judge did not make any reference to why it should be the plaintiff who was terminated, rather than the accounts manager who was employed to replace her while she was on leave.

483 *Ibid.*, at para 4.5.25.

484 *Thomson v. Orica* [2002] FCA 939.

485 *Ibid.*, at para 51.

486 *Ibid.*, at para 150.

487 *Ibid.*, at para 149.

488 *Sheaves v. AAPT Limited* [2006] FMCA 1380 (7 November 2006).

489 *Ibid.*, at para 8.

In the 2017 case of *Mahajan v. Burgess Rawson & Associates Pty Ltd*,[490] the plaintiff, who worked for a real estate company, argued that she was dismissed the day before her probation period expired because she was pregnant and this constituted direct sex discrimination. The defendant claimed that he terminated her employment because she made errors in her work and he was not confident that he could rely on her to produce key documents. Although the judge found the defendant's evidence 'unconvincing', he found that the express reasons the defendant gave for dismissing the plaintiff (the errors in her work and poor punctuality) excluded, by implication, sex discrimination. The judge stated that '[i]t makes no sense' that the employer would have dismissed the plaintiff because she was a woman 'when a few months previously the respondent had employed her, knowing that she was a woman.'[491] Instead, sex discrimination applies 'more naturally' to instances where an employer refuses to hire a person. The court concluded the plaintiff was dismissed because she took personal leave, took annual leave and was temporarily absent from work due to illness or injury.[492]

3.2.1.5 *Workplace Culture*

There have also been cases where plaintiffs have argued that they have been excluded from networking and masculine-orientated events. In these cases, the judges have failed to find any direct sex discrimination[493] despite research illustrating how gender regimes within the workplace are perpetuated through masculine social events that exclude women.[494] In *Shaw v. Perpetual Trustees*,[495] for example, the plaintiff argued that she was excluded from professional lunches, auctions, wage increases and study facilities at work by reason of her sex. Additionally, a ribald cartoon was shown in the office which the plaintiff argued was sex discrimination. The judge was unimpressed with the evidence and could not see any sex discrimination in the defendant's conduct. No one else in the office 'was particularly upset by the presence of the video on the single occasion or the ribald cartoon' and evidence showed

490 *Mahajan v. Burgess Rawson & Associates Pty Ltd* [2017] FCCA 1560.

491 *Ibid.*, at para 55.

492 *Ibid.*, at para 56, 79.

493 *Shaw v. Perpetual Trustees* [1993] HREOCA 19 (10 September 1993).

494 Renate Ortlieb and Barbara Sieben, 'Balls, Barbecues and Boxing: Contesting Gender Regimes, at Organizational Social Events' *Organization Studies* 40(1) (2019), 115–134; and Owen McNamara, '"Making Coin" and the Networker: Masculine Self-making in the Australian Professional Managerial Class' *Australian Journal of Anthropology* 30(3) (2019), 294–308.

495 Shaw, above n. 493.

that junior males were also excluded from social events and 'did not always attend auctions.'[496] Finally, the judge noted that 'all women who were asked gave evidence of improvement in recent times in the office so far as the equality of women was concerned.'[497]

3.2.1.6 *Male Plaintiffs*

The SDA is gender neutral, extending to male victims of sex discrimination. A gender-neutral approach supports the view that while women need equality in the private sphere and access to the public sphere free from discrimination, men also need access to the roles that have been typically ascribed to women.[498] For example, if men do not have access to parental leave then the ability to use the SDA to achieve that right would be in accord with the spirit of sex discrimination law. Cases, however, that involve men seeking access to the gains that women have made towards equality would not be in accord with the goals of sex discrimination law. Examination of cases brought by men indicate most involve men seeking access to advantages women have received to redress historic inequalities.

For example, in *Tully v. Ceridale Pty Ltd.*,[499] a male plaintiff successfully argued direct sex discrimination in the delivery of services when he was charged $5 to enter a nightclub while his female companion was charged only $3.[500] The defendant argued that the differential cover charge was not intended to constitute sex discrimination but rather was to encourage more women to attend because there was a preponderance of men in attendance. 'The preservation of a balance between men and women patrons tended to ensure a more congenial atmosphere and diminished rowdy behaviour.'[501] The court held, however, that it constituted sex discrimination: 'The grant of a discount to a female entrant at the same time as a male entrant is charged the undiscounted price necessarily results in the male entrant being treated less favourably than the female entrant. The underlying intention, whether it be good or bad, is irrelevant. There is therefore no escape from the conclusion that discrimination on the ground of sex occurred.'[502]

496 Shaw, above n. 493.

497 Shaw, above n. 493.

498 Cary Franklin, 'The Anti-Stereotyping Principle in Constitutional Sex Discrimination Law' *New York University Law Review* 85(1) (2010), 83–173.

499 *Tully v. Ceridale Pty Ltd* [1990] HREOCA 6 (19 June 1990).

500 *Ibid.*

501 *Ibid.*

502 *Ibid.*

In *Boase v. ABC*,[503] the male plaintiff successfully argued he was not considered for a position at the ABC because he was male. The defendant had previously stated, prior to the selection process, he preferred a female. There were nine applicants for the job and five were shortlisted for interview. The plaintiff was not one of the five shortlisted despite having a long and varied experience in radio and with experience comparable to the other shortlisted applicants. In finding sex discrimination, the Tribunal stated: 'It certainly was sufficient, as it seems to us, to have stirred the interest of the Committee, particularly when compared with the limited broadcasting experience of at least two of the five persons named on the shortlist.'[504] The plaintiff was therefore treated less favourably than the female applicants and the Tribunal concluded this was 'by reason of' his sex.

In a final example, *Mangan v. Melbourne Cricket Club*,[505] a male plaintiff successfully argued that a cricket club discriminated against him because he was not able to make use of a Rule which enables a member to nominate a female who is on the Waiting List for Full Membership, Intermediate Membership or Junior Membership. The plaintiff wanted to be nominated by his brother who was a member. The defendant argued that the proper comparator to a female on the Waiting List, in the context of the Rule was not a male, but other persons on the waiting list. The judge disagreed. 'I cannot accept this. The proper comparator to a provision requiring a person to be female, to take advantage of a certain rule, is a person who is not female.' The court held that it was therefore direct sex discrimination because 'if he had been a woman the club would have admitted him to full membership pursuant to Rule 5.2(c); but, because he was a man, it did not.'[506]

3.2.2 Indirect Discrimination

The SDA, when enacted in 1984, defined indirect discrimination as when a requirement or condition was imposed on a person 'with which a substantially higher proportion of persons of the opposite sex to the aggrieved person comply or are able to comply which is not reasonable having regard to the circumstances of the case; and with which the aggrieved person does not or is not able to comply.'[507] The legislation was amended in 1995 after a parliamentary review with the intent of making indirect discrimination more accessible. This wording was changed to a condition, requirement or practice 'that has,

503 *Boase v. ABC* [1995] HREOCA 17 (11 July 1995).

504 *Ibid.*, at para 4 (Findings).

505 *Mangan v. Melbourne Cricket Club (Anti-Discrimination)* [2006] VCAT 73.

506 *Ibid.*, at para 8.

507 SDA, s. 59(2)(a)–(c).

or is likely to have, the effect of disadvantaging persons of the same sex as the aggrieved person.'[508] This shifted the focus from technical assessments of disproportionate impact to practices that disadvantages members of a sex.

Additionally, the burden of establishing reasonableness was shifted from the plaintiff to the defendant, embedding it as a defence, and the meaning of reasonableness was set out much more fully although without altering the meaning of reasonableness itself.[509] The amended legislation set out in section 7B a comprehensive overview of what 'reasonableness in the circumstances' means. A person does not discriminate against another person by imposing, or proposing to impose, a condition, requirement or practice that has, or is likely to have, the disadvantaging effect mentioned in subsection 5 'if the condition, requirement or practice is reasonable in the circumstances.'[510] Section 7 further states that the matters to be taken into account in deciding whether a condition, requirement or practice is reasonable in the circumstances include: (a) the nature and extent of the disadvantage resulting from the imposition, or proposed imposition, of the condition, requirement or practice; and (b) the feasibility of overcoming or mitigating the disadvantage; and (c) whether the disadvantage is proportionate to the result sought by the person who imposes, or proposes to impose, the condition, requirement or practice.

Although indirect discrimination claims overall have had limited success, initially there were promising cases after the amendments.[511] In the 1989 of *Secretary of the Department of Foreign Affairs and Trade v. Styles*,[512] the plaintiff argued she was a victim of indirect sex discrimination after she was not considered for a transfer to an overseas posting. The plaintiff applied for the transfer to a London post after it was advertised. There were twelve applicants – two of them Grade A2 journalists, and ten Grade A1 journalists. Grade A1 is immediately below Grade A2 and the plaintiff was a Grade A1 journalist. Although the London position was designated Grade A2, Grade A1 journalists were invited to apply. The approach of the defendant was however that if Grade A2 journalists applied, then Grade A1 were automatically excluded. The plaintiff argued that because women are disproportionately represented amongst Grade A2 journalists, this constituted indirect sex discrimination and this was not 'reasonable in the circumstances.' While the Tribunal found in her favour, this was

508 SDA, s. 5(2).

509 SDA, s. 5(1).

510 SDA, s. 7B.

511 Beth Gaze, 'The Sex Discrimination Act, at 25: Reflections on the Past, Present and Future' in Margaret Thornton (ed.), *Sex Discrimination in Uncertain Times* (ANU, 2010), 107–132.

512 *Secretary of the Department of Foreign Affairs and Trade v. Styles* [1989] FCA 546.

overturned on appeal.[513] The appeal judges found that the test of reasonableness is less demanding than one of necessity, but more demanding than a test of convenience:

> The criterion is an objective one, which requires the court to weigh the nature and extent of the discriminatory effect, on the one hand, against the reasons advanced in favour of the requirement or condition on the other. All the circumstances of the case must be taken into account.[514]

Applying these criteria to the facts, the court held that the practice of appointing officers at their substantive grade is conducive to tidy administration, and it is fair that persons be employed according to the substantive level of their qualification. The court concluded that it might have been more fruitful for the plaintiff to have employed employment law to challenge the failure to consider her as an applicant rather than sex discrimination.[515]

In the 1997 case of *Finance Sector Union v. Commonwealth Bank of Australia*,[516] the plaintiff, under the original wording of the SDA, successfully argued indirect sex discrimination in the Tribunal. The defendant bank was undergoing a major restructure and all positions in the retail section were abolished and new positions created, with a reduction of about 25 percent of the positions. The plaintiff argued two acts of indirect sex discrimination. The first was the failure of the defendant to grant women, who were on extended leave for reasons connected with childbirth or child care, the opportunity to express interest in voluntary retrenchment.[517] The second was that to secure a position in the new structure, a person must be available to take up duties within four weeks of the confirmation of the position, which she argued disadvantaged women who were more likely than men to be on leave associated with child-care.[518]

It was calculated that there was a disparity between men and women of 8–9 percent of those that were excluded from voluntary redundancy and from being able to apply for the new positions. The defendant argued that a disparity between men and women of less than 20 percent is not sufficient to

513 *Ibid.*

514 Stella Tarrant, 'Reasonableness in the Sex Discrimination Act: No Package Deals' *University of Tasmania Law Review* 19(1) (2000), 38–56: 42.

515 *Styles*, above n. 512.

516 *Finance Sector Union v. Commonwealth Bank of Australia* [1997] HREOCA 12 (21 March 1997).

517 *Ibid.*, at 2.

518 *Ibid.*, at 2.1.

constitute a 'substantial difference'.[519] The Tribunal disagreed and held a disparity of 8–9 percent was sufficient to constitute a substantial difference. The defendant also argued even if it did constitute indirect sex discrimination, their position was reasonable because, firstly, it was not commercially viable to leave positions open. Secondly, defendant maintained that it is inconsistent with the Award for officers on extended leave to be invited to express interest in retrenchment if they were not occupying a position which was going to retrenched. Thirdly, approximately 30 percent of women on long leave do not return to work. Finally, defendant argued that those on extended leave were guaranteed a comparable position on their return to work and this entitlement was left unaffected.[520] The Tribunal did not find any of these reasons established reasonableness and therefore the complaint of indirect sex discrimination was made out. On appeal to the Federal Court, however, the judges overturned the decision of the Tribunal finding it had failed to take all circumstances into account. In particular, the court held that the guarantee of re-employment suggested reasonableness.[521]

In the 1998 case of *Hickie v. Hunt & Hunt* as discussed above, the plaintiff who unsuccessfully argued direct sex discrimination was instead successful on her claim of indirect sex discrimination.[522] The plaintiff, who had commenced as a lawyer and then taken maternity leave, returned to find her practice reduced and ultimately her contract was not renewed. Despite not finding direct discrimination the court, intriguingly was much more sympathetic to the claim of indirect sex discrimination.[523] The plaintiff argued that maintaining her practice rested on her not taking maternity leave and not working part-time and this was a condition that more men could comply with, which was not reasonable, and which she could not comply with.[524] The judge agreed and concluded that the removal of the plaintiff's practice by the firm while she was on maternity leave was partly because she intended to work part-time on her return and could not manage such a large practice without supporting staff. Removing her practice, rather than finding other alternatives to maintain it in whole, or in part, was likely more convenient to the firm. However, the judge stated that if part of the motivation to reduce the plaintiff's practice was her intention to work part-time, then this constitutes indirect discrimination since a requirement to work full-time is a requirement with which a substantially

519 *Ibid.*, at 3.

520 *Ibid.*, at 8.2.

521 *Finance Sector Union of Australia v. Commonwealth Bank of Australia* [2002] FCA 1166.

522 *Hickie v. Hunt & Hunt* [1998] HREOCA 8 (9 March 1998).

523 Gaze, above n. 511, 118.

524 *Hickie* above n. 522, at para 4.5.26.

higher proportion of men comply or are able to comply.[525] The judge dismissed the argument by the defendant that even if it were sex discrimination, it was reasonable because 'Hunt and Hunt have accepted that women should be able to work part-time after their maternity leave.' They should have sought alternative solutions which would have enabled her to maintain as much of her practice as possible, the judge concluded.[526] The removal of the plaintiff's plaintiff-practice was therefore an act of indirect discrimination on the grounds of sex within the meaning of the SDA.[527] The different wording of the prohibition on indirect discrimination requiring the effect of disadvantage, rather than 'by reason of sex', appears to have supported the finding that mixed motives was not relevant in indirect discrimination claims despite excluding a claim in direct discrimination.

The plaintiff in *Hickie v. Hunt & Hunt* also argued that narrow male views about management styles, marketing and methods of practice-building constituted indirect sex discrimination. In particular, she argued that marketing activities which involved taking clients to mainly male sporting events or organizing sporting competitions between the firm and clients such as cricket, pool and golf excluded and disadvantaged female employees. She argued she had not been invited to such events and that 'football tipping and touch football were activities in which most females do not participate.' She further complained about the 'bow tie day', which catered to male employees.[528] The defendant argued women were not excluded from these events. The judge did not recognize indirect discrimination despite the clear masculine focus embedded in the various events.[529] Rather, the judge stated, the fact that she did not enjoy the social activities does not mean that she suffered a detriment, such as being made to feel excluded or uncomfortable on the ground of sex.[530] No indirect discrimination was found.[531]

The plaintiff in the 2007 case of *Thompson v. Big Bert Pty Ltd t/as Charles Hotel* unsuccessfully argued indirect sex discrimination.[532] The plaintiff worked as a bar attendant at the defendant's hotel from 1999 until the end of

525 *Hickie* above n. 522, at para 4.5.29.
526 *Hickie* above n. 522, at para 4.5.30.
527 *Hickie* above n. 522, at para 4.5.34.
528 *Hickie*, above n. 522, at para 5.3.2.
529 Deborah Gray, Nancy Hicks and Jennifer Rundels, 'Getting in the Game: Putting Golf, at the Forefront of your Networking Toolbox' Business Horizons 63(5) (2020), 627–636; and LaCalvince Demor Simpson, 'Jacks, Jills, and the Buffalo Bills: Sexism and Unfair Employment Practices in the Workplace' *Journal of Critical Incidents* 11 (2018).
530 *Hickie*, above n. 522, at para 5.3.4.
531 *Hickie*, above n. 522, at para 5.3.5.
532 *Thompson v. Big Bert Pty Ltd t/as Charles Hotel* [2007] FCA 1978; and 168 IR 309.

2005. Initially, she worked mainly fixed and regular shifts but in 2005 her shift arrangements were varied, and she lost both regularity and quantity of work. According to the plaintiff, the defendant had said he wanted to replace some older staff with 'young glamours'. Some of the other female bar staff were the plaintiff's age or older and some were younger.[533] The plaintiff argued indirect sex discrimination on the basis that she was asked to be available to work any shifts in an irregular pattern varying from week to week and lacking any predictability or certainty. That requirement, the plaintiff argued, disproportionately impacts on women because the burden of the care of young children in Australia falls predominantly upon women.[534] The judge rejected her argument on the basis that her children were 6 and 13 years old at the relevant time and she cared for them as a single parent: 'I can see no basis to distinguish her circumstances from that of other single parents. There is no basis for any finding of indirect sex discrimination.'[535] The judge does not engage with the reality that most single parents are women and does not appear to consider the claim of indirect discrimination at all, since it is surely based on the way that the defendants work practices impact on women disproportionately.

The male plaintiff in the 2011 case of *Walker v. Cormack* arrived to participate in a class run at the defendant's gym, knowing the class called 'Women on Weights' was a women-only morning class exercising to music and using small weights.[536] The plaintiff asked the instructor in charge of the class for permission to participate and also asked the female participants whether they objected to him joining them. No-one objected. The plaintiff began to participate in the class but was later removed by the defendant. The judge accepted the exclusion as sex discrimination but held the exclusion was reasonable.[537] On appeal the court did not accept that there was indirect sex discrimination. That determination required an examination of what was available to the plaintiff and how women were treated or would be treated in the same circumstance. Further, it would have been necessary to examine the circumstances in a much broader compass, in order to determine whether the imposition of a requirement or condition or practice that every person attending the Tuesday morning exercise with weights class be female was reasonable.[538]

In the recent 2018 case of *Barnett v. Royal Queensland Golf Club*[539] as discussed above, the plaintiff, unable to complete 18 holes of golf on Wednesdays

533 *Ibid.*, at para 1.
534 *Ibid.*, at para 48.
535 *Ibid.*, at para 50.
536 *Walker v. Cormack* [2011] FCA 861.
537 *Ibid.*, at para 22.
538 *Ibid.*, at para 26.
539 *Barnett v. Royal Queensland Golf Club* [2018] FCCA 3697 (12 December 2018).

due to a men's competition despite that being a guarantee of her membership, successfully argued indirect sex discrimination. The court held, without any extended reasoning, that the restrictions placed upon the plaintiff by the 2016 playing schedule had the effect of disadvantaging females and constituted indirect discrimination.[540] The defendant argued that exclusion of female full members from playing 18 holes of golf on Wednesdays was reasonable in the circumstances and provided the following justifications. The defendant argued that at all material times, there were fewer female members than male members with no explanation as to why this might make the plaintiff's exclusion reasonable). The defendant also maintained that some female and male members were and are not eligible to participate in the Wednesday male-only competition because their category of membership did not allow them to play on Wednesday (although this did not include the plaintiff). The defendant stated that the golf course was not available to members at other times including during course maintenance, special events, championships and corporate events or if there were no tee times left available due to other members booking the times (again no explanation as to how this makes reasonable the regular exclusion of the plaintiff on a Wednesday). The defendant also posited that allowing eligible female members to access the course on Wednesdays during the Wednesday male-only competition would significantly limit the capacity of eligible male members to play in that competition (a separate and unrelated issue) and if eligible female members were able to access the course on Wednesdays during the Wednesday male-only competition it would be necessary for eligible male members to be given access to the course on Tuesdays during female-only competitions limiting the capacity and desire of female members to play in those competitions (however it is unclear why this would be necessary since male full members can already play 18 holes any day of the week without access to Tuesday time slot).[541] The court did not accept any of these reasons as reasonable.[542]

3.3 *The Application of Sex Protection in India*

India is a federation of twenty-eight states and eight union territories as established by the *Constitution of India* 1950 (Constitution). India acceded to the *ICCPR* and *ICESCR* in 1979 and to *CEDAW* in 1993. There are limited avenues for sex discrimination actions in India. The most utilized avenue is through the Constitution, which was adopted several decades before India's ratification of the key conventions.

540 *Ibid.*, at para 35.
541 *Ibid.*, at para 37.
542 *Ibid.*, at para 38.

The Constitution explicitly prohibits sex discrimination in two articles. Article 15 provides a stand-alone prohibition on sex discrimination. Article 15(1) provides that the 'state shall not discriminate against any citizen on grounds only of religion, race, caste, sex, place of birth or any of them.' Article 15(2) provides that:

> [N]o citizen shall, on grounds only of religion, race, caste, sex, place of birth or any of them, be subject to any disability, liability, restriction or condition with regard to (a) access to shops, public restaurants, hotels and palaces of public entertainment; or (b) the use of wells, tanks, bathing ghats, roads and places of public resort maintained wholly or partly out of State funds or dedicated to the use of the general public.

Article 15(1) binds the state and Article 15(2) places a limited 'horizontal' prohibition on sex discrimination by some private actors but does not equate to a prohibition on discrimination by all private individuals and organizations.

Article 16 prohibits sex discrimination 'in matters relating to employment or appointment to any office under the State'. The *Equal Remuneration Act* 1976 additionally prohibits employee sex discrimination with respect to recruitment, wages, work transfers and promotion in the private sector.[543] Finally, Article 14, although it is an equality provision and does not explicitly prohibit sex discrimination, has however been utilized as an avenue for sex discrimination claims.[544]

This section focuses on Article 15(1). The text of Article 15(1) was drafted before the adoption of, and India's accession to, the three conventions that are the focus of this volume. The article does not expressly extend to indirect discrimination and does not set out the elements for determining whether sex discrimination has occurred. Consequently, the interpretation of Article 15 by the Indian courts, in particular the High Courts of each state and the Supreme Court, is important. However, interpretation of Article 15(1) has been restrictive, often even denying direct sex discrimination in many instances, although a recent case may signal a shift towards a more progressive interpretation.[545]

This part has two subsections that take up the interpretation of Article 15(1) by the courts. As indirect discrimination is not a recognized avenue of sex

543 *Equal Remuneration Act* 1976, s. 4.

544 Catharine MacKinnon, 'Sex Equality under the Constitution of India: Problems, Prospects, and Personal Laws' *International Journal of Constitutional Law* 4(2) (2006), 181–202; and Irfan Rasool Najar and Ananya Gupta, 'Special Provisions for Women under the Constitution of India' *Journal of Critical Reviews* 7(9) (2020), 1514–1517.

545 *Navtej Singh Johar & Ors. v. Union of India thr. Secretary Ministry of Law and Justice* Writ Petition (Criminal) No. 76 of 2016, Supreme Court 2018.

discrimination, there is no separate subsection on indirect discrimination as above for the United States and Australia. There is, however, in some of the cases described below, some acknowledgement of indirect discrimination. The first subsection considers the requirement for a similarly-situated comparator of the opposite sex, with a focus on the use of gender-role stereotypes by the courts in many (but not all) cases as evidence of inherent differences between men and women with the result that no male comparator can be identified. The second subsection considers the use of the word 'only' in Article 15(1), its interpretation by the courts to mean that where there is any other factor alongside sex causing differentiation, then it is not sex discrimination. This has resulted in the exclusion of many cases of direct sex discrimination because there are other contributing factors, even when those contributing factors themselves constitute sex discrimination. At the same time, this interpretation of 'only' operates to exclude any consideration of the compounded impact of multiple discriminations.

3.3.1 Opposite-Sex Comparator

The wording of Article 15(1) does not mandate a comparison between similarly-situated women and men to determine whether sex discrimination has occurred. Although the jurisprudence on Article 15(1) is not explicit in adopting a comparator approach, a close reading of the cases indicates that it is an element that must be satisfied to establish sex discrimination. Indeed, from the earliest interpretation of Article 15(1) (in the High Courts and in the Supreme Court), there is a presumed requirement for an opposite-sex similarly-situated comparator treated differently on the ground of sex, in order to establish sex discrimination.

In many cases, as discussed below, the comparator requirement has been utilized by the courts to exclude straightforward situations of direct sex discrimination in law. They have done this by linking the comparator requirement to gender-role stereotypes and socially-constructed differences, and naming them as 'inherent' differences. In these cases, no similarly-situated male comparator is found. While this approach by the Indian courts has made the achievement of formal equality for women difficult, there are exceptional examples where the courts have rejected gender-role stereotypes as evidence of 'difference', and, more recently, a more active acceptance that gender-role stereotypes do not equate to inherent differences between men and women. However, as discussed below, these provide exceptions.

There are few examples of indirect sex discrimination claims, not explicitly protected in Article 15(1), and most of these have been unsuccessful. The opposite-sex comparator requirement often excludes such actions because while typically there is a male comparator, he is treated similarly, not differently by the gender-neutral law and the Indian courts do not investigate or consider impact, which is the heart of an indirect discrimination claim. This section showcases a selection of cases, Supreme Court and High Courts of the different states, from 1950 to 2020 that illustrate the deployment of the comparator requirement in the interpretation of Article 15(1). Most of the cases are direct sex discrimination actions, although a few are indirect sex discrimination actions. The cases illustrate how the opposite-sex comparator requirement has operated to deny many deserving actions, but also show a gradual evolution towards a more contemporary approach.

Four years after the Constitution was adopted but prior to the adoption and accession to relevant international conventions, the male petitioner in the 1954 case of *Yusuf Abdul Aziz v. State of Bombay*,[546] who was being prosecuted for adultery, argued that s. 497 of the Indian *Penal Code* 1860, which criminalizes men but not women, was sex discrimination and should be voided.[547] The High Court of Bombay, denying the claim, and relying on a raft of gender-role stereotypes, stated:

> Women from the point of view of sex and femininity are the same all the world over, but surely it cannot be said that women all the world over share the affection of their husbands with their rivals or that they are secluded or that they are married when they are in their cradle or when they are children. Therefore what led to this discrimination in this country is not the fact that women had a sex different from that of men, but that women in this country were so situated that special legislation was required in order to protect them, and it was from this point of view that one finds in s. 497 a position in law which takes a sympathetic and charitable view of the weakness of women in this country.[548]

The Supreme Court affirmed the decision.[549] At the heart of the court's reasoning is a perception of women without agency who are victims of men's adulterous behaviour. Although this outcome may have been beneficial to many women, it is underscored by flawed-reasoning based on gender stereotypes and a finding that there is no similarly-situated male comparator. Women and men are 'inherently' different because of their weakness and therefore no comparison between men and women can be made.

546 *Yusuf Abdul Aziz v. State of Bombay*, AIR 1951 Bom 470 (1951).

547 *Ibid.*, at para 1.

548 *Ibid.*, at para 5.

549 *Yusuf Abdul Aziz v. State of Bombay*, 1954 AIR 32 (1954).

However, although all courts have adopted an opposite-sex comparator approach, there are examples from the earliest interpretation of Article 15(1) where the courts have rejected gender-role stereotypes and held instead that an opposite-sex comparator can be identified. For example, also in 1954 but in direct contrast to *Yusuf Abdul Aziz*, the court facing similar issues reached a different conclusion. In *Rani Raj Rajeshwari Devi v. The State of U.P. and Ors*,[550] the petitioner, a widow, was declared unfit to manage her estates under Clause 8(1)(b) of the *Court of Wards Act* 1879 (U.P.) which classes as 'disqualified proprietors' 'females declared by the Local Government to be incapable of managing their own property'.[551] The Local Government of Uttar Pradesh thus has the discretion under the legislation (subjective and non-justiciable) to declare a female proprietor unfit to manage her estate without any rules to guide it in determining what constitutes incapacity to manage.[552] A male, however in contrast, cannot be declared unfit to manage his estate unless certain conditions are met. Additionally, a male, but not a female, must be given the fullest opportunity to have his objections heard.[553] The defendant argued in support of the (unequal) provision 'it is a well-known fact that women generally are not such competent managers of property as men and are much more liable to be led astray and, therefore, for the purposes of management of property, they may legitimately be put in a class by themselves.'[554] The court, however, rejected the gender-role stereotypes held up by the defendant, and held that men and women could not be regarded as separate classes merely through the attribution of characteristics to all men (competent managers of property) and all women (incompetent managers of property).[555] It concluded that Article 15(1) was violated because although 'the law may be a benign one, there can be no doubt that the discrimination is against the female.'[556] Thus although a comparator requirement was employed this court did not, in contrast to *Yusuf Abdul Aziz*, rely on a gender-role stereotype of women as incompetent managers of property (although the State of U.P. argued it should) to find that no similarly-situated male could be identified with whom to compare the petitioner.[557]

550 *Rani Raj Rajeshwari Devi v. The State of U.P. and Ors*, AIR All 608 (1954).
551 *Court of Wards Act* (U.P.) 1879, s. 8(1)(b).
552 *Ibid.*
553 *Ibid.*, at s. 8(1)(d).
554 *Rani Raj Rajeshwari Devi*, above n. 551, at para 57.
555 *Rani Raj Rajeshwari Devi*, above n. 551, at para 58.
556 *Rani Raj Rajeshwari Devi*, above n. 551, at para 58.
557 *Rani Raj Rajeshwari Devi*, above n. 551, at para 56.

Gender-role stereotypes were, however, again successfully deployed by the State of Punjab in the 1976 case of *R.S Singh v. State of Punjab*[558] to support a finding that no similarly-situated male comparator could be identified. The petitioner argued that a Governor's order disqualifying women from being appointed to posts in a men's jail (apart from as a clerk or as a matron) was sex discrimination.[559] The court agreed with the State of Punjab that there are certain 'inherent and natural' differences between the sexes: 'That there are patent physical disparities between the two sexes is so obvious that it would be platitudinous to advert to them in detail.'[560] These perceived physical disparities led the court to conclude that there could be no 'similarly-situated' male comparator:

> It needs no great imagination to visualise the awkward and even the hazardous position of a woman acting as a warder or other jail official who has to personally ensure and maintain discipline over habitual male criminals. Necessarily the inmates of these jails have a majority of hardened and ribald criminals guilty of heinous crimes of violence and sex. The duties of the Superintendent and his subordinate officials and warders involve a direct and continuous contact with these inmates. The difficulties which even male warders and other jail officials experience in handling this motley and even dangerous assemblage are too clear to need elaboration. A woman performing these duties in a men's jail would be even in a more hazardous predicament.[561]

The court, although focussing on perceived physical differences between men and women, actually identifies in large part perceived non-physical differences, amounting to gender-role stereotypes, for example, women's inability to control male inmates and the danger that female, but not male, warders would face from dangerous criminals because of their perceived weakness, fragility and vulnerability.

In the 1981 Supreme Court case of *Air India v. Nergesh Meerza.*[562] female flight attendants argued the Air India *Employees Service Regulations* and the Indian Airlines *Service Regulations* which provided that women's employment

558 *Raghubans Saudagar Singh v. The State of Punjab and Or*, AIR 1972 P& H 117.

559 *Ibid.*, at para 2.

560 *Ibid.*, at para 9.

561 *Ibid.*, at para 17.

562 *Air India v. Nergesh Meerza and Ors, AIR* SC 1829 (1981).

for Air India and Indian Airlines terminated upon reaching the age of 35 years (but not men's), or upon marriage if within four years of service (but not men's), or upon the first pregnancy, constituted sex discrimination.[563] Air India and Indian Airlines argued that the job functions performed by flight pursers (male) and air hostesses (female) are entirely different and therefore, as they constituted two different classes of employees that were governed by two different sets of service conditions, no legitimate comparison could be made.[564] The Supreme Court agreed, reasoning the 'inescapable conclusion that follows is that ... there are two separate and different classes having different conditions of service and different incidents, [and] the question of discrimination does not arise.'[565] On early retirement, the Supreme Court stated:

> Duties in air are full of tension and sometimes hazardous. They have, therefore, agreed for comparatively early age of retirement with option to accept duties on the ground. There is nothing objectionable for air hostesses to wish for a peaceful and tension-free life at home with their families in the middle age and avoid remaining away for long durations on international flights.[566]

On the condition that the employment would be terminated if an air hostess married within four years of joining, the Supreme Court noted:

> So far as the question of marriage within four years is concerned, we do not think that the provisions suffer from any constitutional infirmity. ... there are very few who decide to marry immediately after entering the service ... the Regulation permits (her) to marry at the age of 23 if she has joined the service at the age of 19 which is by all standards a very sound and salutary provision. Apart from improving the health of the employee, it helps in the boosting up of our family planning programme. Secondly, if a woman marries near about the age of 20 to 23 years, she becomes fully mature and there is every chance of such a marriage proving a success, all things being equal. Thirdly, it has been rightly pointed out to us by

563 *Ibid.*
564 *Ibid.*
565 *Ibid.*
566 *Ibid.*

> the Corporation that if the bar of marriage within four years of service is removed then the Corporation will have to incur huge expenditure ...[567]

Only on the issue of termination of employment for a first pregnancy did the Supreme Court recognize (some limited) sex discrimination. 'It seems to us that the termination of the services of an air hostess under such circumstances is not only a callous and cruel act but an open insult to Indian womanhood the most sacrosanct and cherished institution.'[568] The Supreme Court proposed replacing 'first pregnancy' with 'third pregnancy' and imposed a series of requirements on air hostesses, such as taking leave without pay during the pregnancy period and having to undergo an annual fitness examination 'in the interests of maintenance of efficiency'.[569] The decision was upheld in 2003.[570] The Supreme Court concluded therefore that male pursers and female air hostesses are not similarly situated and treated differently on the ground of sex, but rather that they are differently situated, and no male comparator can be identified. In coming to this conclusion, the court relies on a raft of gender-role stereotypes, including that women, but not men, have domestic responsibilities which mean they are not suited to being away from home on long flights and schedules, that marriage is dependent on women's, but not men's maturity, and this will likely occur between the ages of 20 and 23, and, finally, that Indian womanhood is sacred and cherished and must be protected, but no similar finding in relation to Indian manhood. In sum, three examples of straightforward direct sex discrimination are characterized as not violative of Article 15(1).[571]

In the 2000 case of *Vasantha R. v. Union of India & Ors*,[572] in a finding similar to *Rani* discussed above, the Punjab-Haryana High Court refused to rely on gender-role stereotypes. The petitioner, who was a worker in a textile mill in Dharmapuri District that undertook spinning, weaving, processing and printing, was unable to work any night shifts because of a provision in the *Factories Act* 1948 which banned women from working between 7:00 p.m. and 6:00 a.m. She argued that the provision, although purporting to protect women from a raft of 'dangers', was based on gender-role stereotypes and violated

567 *Ibid.*

568 *Ibid.*

569 *Ibid.*

570 *Air India Cabin Crew Association v. Yashaswinee Merchant* 2003 6 SCC 277.

571 Kalpana Kannabiran, 'Judicial Meanderings in Patriarchal Thickets: Litigating Sex Discrimination in India' *Economic and Political Weekly* (2009), 88–98: 91.

572 *Vasantha R. v. Union of India (Uoi) And Ors* IILLJ 843 Mad I (2001).

Article 15(1).[573] The Punjab-Haryana state argued the restriction 'is to protect the female workers from exploitation and it is for their interest and safety. It is a special provision to safeguard the interest of the weaker section'[574] and 'if the women are required or allowed to work during the night shifts, it would result in their being subjected to very strenuous work as in addition to their working in factories they have to attend to their household duties.'[575] Additionally the defendant argued, any relaxation of the provision 'may lead to employment of a single woman worker to mingle with group of male workers during night hours.'[576] The Punjab-Haryana High Court disagreed, finding that 'there is no difference at all between a male worker and a female worker.'[577] 'Excepting the solitary reason, namely difference in sex among the workers, there is no reason or rhyme to treat the women differently, nor it could be held that it is a protective legislation to save the women from exploitation. On the other hand, the very provision results in denial of livelihood, improvement in status to women as well as economic freedom and the impugned provision in any view of the matter offends Article 15(1) of the Constitution.'[578] The court therefore found men and women to be similarly situated, treated differently, and did not accept the gender-role stereotypes as 'inherent differences' as argued by the defendant.

The petitioners challenged new amendments to the Maharashtra Police Act 1951, *Police Act* 1951, in the 2006 case of *Indian Hotel and Restaurant Association v. State of Maharashtra and Others*.[579] The amendments cancelled licences and prohibited 'holding of a performance of dance, of any kind or type, in any eating house, permit room or beer bar'.[580] The petitioners, who were female bar dancers, argued that women constitute an overwhelming majority of bar dancers and that the primary object, and the direct and inevitable effect, of the prohibition of dance performance in dance bars is the disproportionate denial of employment opportunities to women. This was, they argued, sex discrimination under Article 15(1)[581] despite the legislation 'being couched in facially neutral language.'[582] In effect, the petitioners were calling on the

573 *Ibid.*, at para 10.
574 *Ibid.*, at para 24.
575 *Ibid.*, at para 53.
576 *Ibid.*, at para 25, 53.
577 *Ibid.*, at para 73.
578 *Ibid.*, at para 55.
579 *Indian Hotel and Restaurant Association v. State of Maharashtra and Others* 2006 Bom CR 705.
580 *Maharashtra Police Act* 1951 s. 33A, 33B.
581 Indian Hotel, above n. 579, at para 24.
582 Indian Hotel, above n. 579, at para 24.

Bombay High Court to recognize indirect sex discrimination, an ambitious claim given that the judiciary had struggled previously to recognize even direct sex discrimination. The Bombay High Court (perhaps predictably) held that the law banning dancing in some establishments and exempting other establishments:

> [I]s not traceable to banning dances performed by women only. Although the preamble, the objects and reasons clause, to the amendment and the reply of the State, indicates that it is to ban dancing by women, that, however, does not mean that dancing is being prohibited only on the ground of sex. What is being prohibited is dancing in identified establishments. No dancing is permitted in the establishments say by males.[583]

The court went on to conclude:

> The argument could have been accepted if in the banned establishments dancing by males were permitted. The law makes no such distinction. The Act prohibits all types of dances in the banned establishments by any person or persons ... The prohibition, therefore, applies to both men and women. That being the case, the argument advanced on behalf of the petitioners of violation of Article 15(1) has no merits and consequently must be rejected.[584]

On appeal to the Supreme Court, the unfavourable decision was overturned on the basis that the law violated Article 14 and bar dancing was reinstated.[585] In relation to Article 15(1) the Supreme Court noted however: 'We make it very clear that we have not expressed any opinion on the correctness or otherwise of the conclusions of the High Court with regard to Sections 33A and 33B (of the Bombay Police Act) not being ultra vires Articles 15(1).'[586] Thus, although the petitioners ultimately won through the exercise of Article 14, their Article 15(1) action failed in the Bombay High Court and the Supreme Court. The 'neutral' ban precluded any argument that there was sex discrimination in breach of Article 15(1), because although there was a male comparator, he was treated in the same way as the women and therefore it was not sex discrimination.

583 Indian Hotel, above n. 579, at para 24.
584 Indian Hotel, above n. 579, at para 24.
585 *Indian Hotel and Restaurant v. The State of Maharashtra* (17 January 2019) Supreme Court of India, Writ Petition No. 24 of 2017, at para 103, 104.
586 Ibid.

The 2007 Supreme Court case of *Anuj Garg and ors v. Hotel Association of India and Ors*[587] signalled a significant shift in the approach of the courts to the use of gender-role stereotypes to support findings that the inherent differences between men and women mean there is no opposite-sex comparator. The Supreme Court upheld a decision of the Delhi High Court that a provision of the *Punjab Excise Act* 1914, which prohibited the employment of 'any woman' in any part of premises in which liquor or intoxicating drug is consumed by the public, is sex discrimination.[588] In coming to this finding, the court dismissed the use of gender-role stereotypes as providing evidence of inherent differences between men and women.[589] The court favourably noted a statement made a decade earlier by United States Supreme Court Justice Ginsburg:

> Inherent differences between men and women, we have come to appreciate, remain cause for celebration, but not for denigration of the members of either sex or for artificial constraints on an individual's opportunity. Sex classifications may be used to compensate women for particular economic disabilities [they have] suffered, to promote equal employment opportunity, to advance full development of the talent and capacities of our Nation's people. But such classifications may not be used, as they once were, to create or perpetuate the legal, social, and economic inferiority of women.[590]

The court did not accept that women faced security issues in premises in which liquor or intoxicating drug is consumed by the public because they are 'inherently' different to men:

> Instead of prohibiting women employment in the bars altogether the state should focus on factoring in ways through which unequal consequences of sex differences can be eliminated. It is state's duty to ensure circumstances of safety which inspire confidence in women to discharge the duty freely in accordance to the requirements of the profession they choose to follow.[591]

587 *Anuj Garg and Ors v. Hotel Association of India and Ors* (2007) 3 SCC 1.

588 *Ibid.*, at para 55.

589 *Ibid.*, at para 43.

590 *Ibid*, quoting Justice Ginsburg, at para 50.

591 *Ibid.*, at para 41.

The Supreme Court concluded that 'in the instant case the end result is an invidious discrimination perpetuating sexual difference.'[592]

In the 2010 case of *R.S.Kavitha v. The State of Tamil Nadu*,[593] the petitioners argued they were denied employment as conductors by the Tamil Nadu state in breach of Article 15(1) because they were women.[594] The defendant advertised conductor posts in its transport corporations. The petitioners, who were unemployed women who had completed a Bachelor of Commerce Degree, had the required physical fitness and had obtained a conductor licence, applied and were interviewed but did not receive the positions and were never notified that they had not been appointed. There were 930 vacancies for the post of conductors out of which 925 posts were allotted to male candidates and only four posts were allotted to women candidates. The first petitioner was not offered employment, according to the defendant, because the Rules state a candidate must have height of 160 cm, and she had only a height of 157 cm.[595] The second petitioner was also not offered employment. She had the requisite qualifications and height, but she had not produced a valid First Aid Certificate at the time of interview.[596] The court did not explicitly examine the indirect discrimination that the height requirement likely presented. Instead, the court examined the validity of a height requirement in general terms and found there was no obvious reason why a person of 157 cm could not perform the job as a bus conductor:[597]

> I am not satisfied with the reason adduced that lacking of 3 cms height than the required height of 160 cms will be detrimental to a lady conductor to perform her function efficiently. The case on hand is not that of physical deformity and is a case of an unemployed woman eager to work by coming out of the traditional bond of homemaker which has to be necessarily supported, strengthened, encouraged and appreciated by the Government and other constitutional authorities.[598]

A successful challenge was made to the validity of s. 497 of the Indian *Penal Code* that restricts the offence of adultery to a man who has sexual relations with married woman 'without the consent or connivance' of her husband

592 *Ibid.*, at para 53.

593 *R.S. Kavitha v. The State of Tamil Nadu* 2010 INDLAW MAD 933.

594 *Ibid.*, at para 2.2.

595 *Ibid.*, at para 3.3.

596 *Ibid.*, at para 3.4.

597 *Ibid.*, at para 13.

598 *Ibid.*, at para 15.

in the 2018 case of *Joseph Shine v. Union of India*.[599] Using a straightforward comparison between men and women, the court held that the adultery provision 'discriminates against women on grounds of sex only and must be struck down on this ground as well.'[600] The court also held that the offence 'treats the woman as a chattel. It treats her as the property of man and totally subservient to the will of the master. It is a reflection of the social dominance that was prevalent when the penal provision was drafted.'[601] Although Article 14 was also used to come to this determination, the decision indicates a movement away from a strict comparator approach to one grounded in the subordination of women.

3.3.2 'Only of' Sex: Causation

The text of Article 15(1) has frustrated the courts' ability to recognize even straightforward examples of direct sex discrimination because of the wording 'the state shall not discriminate against any citizen on grounds only of ...sex.' The judiciary has interpreted the word 'only' to mean that if there are other factors alongside sex that cause differentiation between women and men it is not sex discrimination within the meaning of Article 15(1).[602] When sex combines or intersects with other factors, such as ownership of property, social norms, or different conditions of service as discussed in the cases below, that combination operates to remove the case from the purview of Article 15(1).[603] However, the Supreme Court has recently taken a different approach to the interpretation of the term 'only', heralding both the possibility of greater recognition of direct sex discrimination and also the possibility of an understanding of the nuances of multiple discrimination.[604]

The courts, soon after the adoption of the Constitution, reduced Article 15(1) to prohibiting discrimination only if it is solely on the ground of sex. This has directly led to the denial of many instances of direct sex discrimination and the exclusion of any case where there are multiple discriminations. The

---

599 *Joseph Shine v. Union of India* 2018 SC 1676.

600 *Ibid.*, at para 9.

601 *Ibid.*, at para 23, 25 as per R.F. Nariman.

602 Shreya Atrey, 'Through the Looking Glass of Intersectionality: Making Sense of Indian Discrimination Jurisprudence under Article 15' *The Equal Rights Review* 16 (2016), 160–185: 164.

603 Kannabiran, above n. 571, 337

604 Gautam Bhatia, 'Case Comment: Navtej Singh Johar v. Union of India: The Indian Supreme Court's Decriminalization of Same-Sex Relations' *Max Planck Yearbook of United Nations Law Online* 22(1) (2019), 218–233; and Pratik Dixit, 'Navtej Singh Johar v. Union of India: Decriminalising India's Sodomy Law' *The International Journal of Human Rights* 24(8) (2019), 1–20.

female petitioner in the 1951 case of *Sri Mahadeb Jiew And Anr. v. Dr BB Sen*[605] was required to provide monetary security under the *Civil Procedure Code* 1908 that enables the court (in a civil suit) to demand monetary security from a woman, but not a man, who does not possess sufficient immovable property in India. The petitioner argued the provision constituted sex discrimination since it placed a burden on her that could not be placed on a man.[606] The court agreed that there was sex discrimination but held that there was another contributing factor that determined the outcome – whether a female held sufficient immoveable property in India.[607] This contributing factor meant that the discrimination was not 'only' on the ground of sex and therefore outside the ambit of Article 15(1). Justice Mukherji stated:

> The State shall not discriminate against any citizen on grounds only of sex. The word "only"' in this Article is of great importance and significance which should not be missed. The impugned law must be shown to discriminate because of sex alone. If other factors in addition to sex come into play in making the discriminatory law, then such discrimination does not, in my judgment, come within the provision of Article 15(1) of the Constitution.[608]

Therefore, the word 'only' meant that the sex discrimination could not be actioned because it was accompanied by a further requirement – holding immovable property – which was not based on sex according to the court since presumably some women could meet the requirement.

This reductive approach was again replicated the following year in *Anjali Roy v. State of West Bengal*.[609] The petitioner was a female student of the Hooghly Mohsin College and after passing her second year of study, she applied for the third-year class with Honours in Economics. She was informed, however, that a newly issued order barred the admission of girls beyond the second year. Instead, she was referred to a newly established women's college in Chinsurah, which did not offer Honours and Science subjects and had poor educational facilities. She was, however, permitted to travel back to Hooghly Mohsin College to join classes not offered at the new women's college.[610] The object behind the scheme was, according to Hooghly Mohsin College, to promote the

605 *Sri Mahadeb Jiew And Anr. v. Dr BB Sen* AIR 1951 Cal 563.
606 *Ibid.*, at para 27.
607 *Ibid.*, at para 28, 29, 30.
608 *Ibid.*, at para 28.
609 *Anjali Roy v. State of West Bengal* AIR 1952 Cal 822.
610 *Ibid.*, at para 2.

development of the new college for women and ultimately to make it a well-established and self-sufficient organization for the education of women. The court held she was not refused admission simply 'because she was a woman.'[611] Rather, although it was her sex that prevented her admission, it was coupled with a scheme for women students, 'which covered development of women's college as a step towards the advancement of female education.'[612] This meant the presence of an additional factor (coupled with its positive intent) overrode the sex discrimination which was clearly embedded in the arrangement.

In the 1953 case of *Dattatraya Moriram More v. State of Bombay*,[613] the court examined the provisions of the *Bombay Municipal Boroughs Act* 1925 which reserved four seats for women out of the 35 elected seats for the Jalgaon Municipality. The male petitioner argued the reserved seats constituted sex discrimination.[614] The defendant successfully argued, utilizing the same argument that had benefited men in previous cases under Article 15(1), that any discrimination:

> [I]s not only on the ground that they are women, but there are various other considerations which have come into play. It is said that even today women are more backward than men. It is the duty of the State to raise the position of women to that of men.[615]

The court agreed that it was sex discrimination as in *Anjali Roy* but not 'only' on the basis of sex as it was coupled with other positive objectives.[616]

The next year in *Rani Raj Rajeshwari Devi v. The State of U.P. And Ors*,[617] a widow (as discussed above) was declared unfit to manage her estates under the *Court of Wards Act* 1879 which classed as 'disqualified proprietors' 'females declared by the Local Government to be incapable of managing their own property.'[618] The court rejected the argument of the defendant that if there is discrimination, it was based not 'only' upon the sex of the person concerned but also upon the satisfaction of the Government that the person was incapable of managing her property.[619] The court stated: 'The fact that Government

611 *Ibid.*, at para 3.
612 *Ibid.*, at para 15.
613 *Dattatraya Moriram More v. State of Bombay* AIR 1953 Bom 311.
614 *Ibid.*, at para 1.
615 *Ibid.*, at para 7.
616 *Ibid.*, at para 7.
617 *Rani Raj Rajeshwari Devi v. The State of U.P. And Ors* AIR 1954 All 608.
618 *Ibid.*, at para 57.
619 *Ibid.*, at para 56.

chooses to proceed in respect of an estate under section 8(1)(b) of the Court of Wards Act is based only on the sex of the proprietor.'[620] While the finding is successful, it does reinforce the requirement that the discrimination must be 'only' on the basis of sex. It is also hard to differentiate this case from the unsuccessful cases that preceded it. For example, in *Mahalebs* an incapacity to own immovable property was regarded as a further factor.

In the 1955 case of *Bombay v. Bombay Education Society*,[621] (although not a case grounded in sex discrimination) a new policy restricted admission to English-speaking students, specifically of Anglo-Indian and European descent, in the English medium schools across Bombay. The petitioner, a member of the Indian Christian Community, was unable to enrol into Barnes High School, an English Medium school. She was denied admission since she did not belong to the Anglo-Indian community and was not of European descent, although she had all the necessary academic qualifications for admission.[622] A second petitioner, a member of the Guzrati Hindu Community, was unable to enrol his son, although he had the necessary qualifications for admission, for the same reason.[623] The defendant argued that the policy does not deny pupils who are not Anglo-Indians or citizens of European descent admission into an Anglo-Indian School 'only on the ground of religion, race, caste, language or any of them' but also on the ground that 'such denial will promote the advancement of the national language and facilitate the imparting of education through the medium of the pupil's mother tongue.'[624] The court disagreed with this argument finding for the petitioner: 'Whatever the object, the immediate ground and direct cause for the denial is that the mother tongue of the pupil is not English.'[625] The court focused in its findings on whether the discriminatory effect was based on any or more than one of the prohibited grounds not whether the purpose of the differentiation was discriminatory or beneficial.[626]

The male petitioner in the 1976 case of *Walter Alfred Baid v. Union of India*[627] was a qualified 'A' grade male nurse who was appointed as 'sister tutor' in the School of Nursing, Irwin Hospital New Delhi. After a period in this role, he challenged Lady Irwin's Hospital Recruitment Rules that permitted only women to

620 *Ibid.*, at para 58.
621 *Bombay v. Bombay Education Society* 1955 1 SCR 568, at 581, 583–584.
622 *Ibid.*
623 *Ibid.*
624 *Ibid.*
625 *Ibid.*
626 Shreya Atrey, 'Through the Looking Glass of Intersectionality: Making Sense of Indian Discrimination Jurisprudence under Article 15' *Equal Rights Review* 16 (2016), 160–185: 166.
627 *Walter Alfred Baid v. Union of India* AIR 1976 Del 302.

be further promoted as a senior nursing tutor.[628] The defendant argued that the rule was not based on sex alone, but on the respective 'suitability' of male and female candidates for the job.[629] The School of Nursing, the defendant argued, is a predominantly female institution, and the duties of the senior tutor make it proper 'that such a post was "manned" by a member of the female sex and the male members of the staff are made ineligible for it for administrative reasons and claims of propriety.'[630] The defendant further argued:

> The ineligibility is not because the male members of the staff belong to that sex but because of the implications of their belonging to that sex. It is, therefore, contended that the ineligibility and discrimination in the present case is permissible because it is not on ground of sex alone but on other considerations.[631]

Rejecting the argument of the defendant, the court held that 'it is difficult to accept the position that a discrimination based on sex is nevertheless not a discrimination based on sex "alone" because it is based on "other considerations" even though these other considerations have their genesis in the sex itself':[632]

> If a person is considered ineligible for a post, whether a male or a female because such a person is too cowardly or too much of a weakling, whether of body or mind, or is of such a frail constitution that there is something in his or her background which makes him or her eminently unsuitable for a particular type of work, it would be within the area of permissible discrimination but where it is stated that, having regard to the physical disparity between the two sexes or the inherent characteristics or susceptibilities of one or the other of the sexes, all members of that or the other sex are ineligible for a particular position, on what else is such discrimination or disability based, if not sex alone?[633]

While it is true 'that there are patent physical disparities between the two sexes, yet it is not possible to justify a conclusion by any process of reasoning, without impinging on the guarantee against discrimination on the ground of sex, that all women or all men, as the case may be, would be unfit or, to put

628 *Ibid.*, at para 2.
629 *Ibid.*, at para 4.
630 *Ibid.*, at para 9.
631 *Ibid.*, at para 10.
632 *Ibid.*, at para 10.
633 *Ibid.*, at para 10.

it differently, no man or woman, as the case may be, would be suitable for a particular class of work.'

Petitioners in the 1995 case of *A.M. Shaila and Ors v. Chairman Cochin Port Trust and Others*[634] were women who were excluded from being employed as shed clerks by the defendant. The defendant argued that they do not employ women because the work is hazardous and because of the 'sensitiveness of their sex and peculiarities of social factors.'[635] The court responded:

> If women are excluded from employment of a particular category because of their physical structure and special susceptibilities it means that women have been placed in a class by reason of the distinct circumstances. In such a case the denial of opportunity of employment, though it strikes at women ceases to be 'solely' on the ground of sex.[636]

The policy of the defendant the court stated indeed 'protects women from the hazardous effect of such work on their well-being. Therefore, the policy is not based only on sex.'[637] The circular reasoning depends on gender-role stereotypes – that women are physically weaker than men, that they have fragile health and that the 'menacing movement of cranes and forklifts' is a danger to them – yet those very gender-role stereotypes mean, according to the court, that the differentiation is based not 'only' on sex but on other characteristics even although they believe the other characteristics to be exclusively associated with women.

In the 2008 case of *Air India v. Nergesh Meerza*[638] (described above), where air hostesses challenged the validity of the *Employees Service Regulations* which provided that their employment terminated upon reaching 35; or on marriage if within 4 years of service; or upon the first pregnancy Air India argued there was no violation of Article 15(1) because the discrimination was not merely based on sex but was 'swayed by a lot of other considerations' including allowances, conditions of service and other types of remuneration.[639] The court agreed, holding that Article 15(1) does 'not prohibit the State from making discrimination on the ground of sex coupled with other considerations.'[640]

634 *A.M. Shaila and Ors v. Chairman Cochin Port Trust and Others* (1995) IILLJ 1193 Ker.
635 *Ibid.*, at para 4.
636 *Ibid.*, at para 8.
637 *Ibid.*, at para 14.
638 *Air India v. Nergesh Meerza* 1982 (2008) 3 SCC 1.
639 *Ibid.*
640 *Ibid.*

The use of the term 'only' to deny sex discrimination if there are other causative factors, coupled with the approach of the judiciary to regard gender-role stereotypes as evidence of inherent differences between women and men, has denied many straightforward instances of direct sex discrimination. As Jaising asserts: 'The use of the word "only" in this Article has enabled the courts to segregate sex from gender and uphold blatantly discriminatory legislation.'[641]

A recent decision in 2018, however, may have shifted the interpretation of 'only'.[642] *Navtej Singh Johar & Ors. v. Union of India thr. Secretary Ministry of Law and Justice* is a landmark decision of the Supreme Court that decriminalized all consensual sex among adults, including same-sex relations.[643] Importantly, Justice Chandrachud in a concurring opinion held that 'discrimination that is a result of grounds rooted in sex and other considerations, can no longer be held to be a position supported by the intersectional understanding of how discrimination operates.'[644] He further stated:

> A provision challenged as being ultra vires the prohibition of discrimination on the grounds only of sex under Article 15(1) is to be assessed not by the objects of the state in enacting it, but by the effect that the provision has on affected individuals and on their fundamental rights. Any ground of discrimination, direct or indirect, which is founded on a particular understanding of the role of the sex, would not be distinguishable from the discrimination which is prohibited by Article 15 on the grounds only of sex.[645]

This opinion suggests that the interpretation of only in Article 15(1) cannot be used to exclude examples of direct sex discrimination on the basis that there were other factors, not related to sex which also cause the discrimination.[646]

---

641 Indira Jaising, 'Gender Justice and the Supreme Court' in B. Kirpal (ed.), *Supreme But not Infallible: Essays in Honour of the Supreme Court of India* (Oxford India Paperbacks, 2000); and Martha Nussbaum, 'India Sex Equality and Constitutional Law' in Beverly Baines and Ruth Rubio-Marin (eds.), *Constituting Women: The Gender of Constitutional Jurisprudence* (Cambridge University Press, 2004), 174–204: 180.

642 *Navtej Singh Johar & Ors. v. Union of India thr. Secretary Ministry of Law and Justice* Writ. Petition (Criminal) No. 76 of 2016, Supreme Court 2018.

643 *Ibid.*, at para 253.

644 *Ibid.*, at para 46.

645 *Ibid.*, at para 41.

646 Pawan Renu, 'Homosexuality with Special Reference Case: Navtej Singh Johar v. Union of India' (2019); and Dominic McGoldrick, 'Challenging the Constitutionality of Restrictions on Same-Sex Sexual Relations: Lessons from India' *Human Rights Law Review* 19(1) (2019),

Part 4: Comparing International and Domestic Sex Discrimination Law

This final part compares the approaches of the three treaty-bodies, and the conventions they monitor, to resolving sex discrimination claims. This part also compares the approaches of the three country-examples to each other and to the international law framework. Through this comparison this part seeks to highlight both the potential and the limitations of sex discrimination law to further gender equality and advance the rights of women.

There are similarities in the treaty-body jurisprudence on sex discrimination, but also differences in their respective interpretations reflecting both the evolution of their approaches over time and the revolving nature of their membership which results in different perspectives entering the decision-making arena. There are also differences between majority decisions and dissenting opinions. The *ICCPR* and *ICESCR*, in their text, do not define the term 'sex discrimination' nor explain what constitutes sex discrimination.[647] *CEDAW* provides a much fuller definition of 'sex discrimination' in Article 1. However, the limited guidance in the text of the three conventions means that it is their jurisprudence that generates the primary commentary on their respective approaches to sex discrimination.

There are similarities and differences in the legal avenues of sex discrimination protection of the United States, Australia and India examined in this volume in the way each country approaches sex discrimination claims as well as differences in their level of adherence to the standards set by the international law framework. In India the text of Article 15(1) of the Constitution falls short of the definition of sex discrimination in *CEDAW*, however it was drafted before the adoption of, and India's accession to, any of the three conventions that are the focus of this volume. The article does not expressly extend to indirect discrimination and does not set out the elements for determining whether sex discrimination has occurred. Title VII in the United States and the SDA in Australia contain much more comprehensive texts on sex discrimination, expressly extending to protection from indirect sex discrimination. In all three countries, however, the decision-making in the tribunals and courts has led to a sex discrimination legal framework that is much more restrictive than the international law framework.

173–185, Poonam Borah, 'Engaging with the Law: Decriminalisation of Homosexuality and the Johar Judgement, 2018' *Space and Culture, India* 6(3) (2018), 5–22.

647 Catalina-Ariana Ivanus, 'Prohibition of Gender Discrimination in Some International Regulations' *Agora International Journal of Juridical Science* 1 (2014), 59–65: 59.

The following sections compare the different approaches by the different jurisdictions (international and domestic) to key issues including the scope of the ground of sex, the use of an opposite-sex-comparator to determine direct discrimination, the requirement of intent to discriminate as an element of direct discrimination, the limited recognition of multiple discrimination in the international context and its absence in the domestic frameworks. In relation to all these key issues, the following sections consider the ways in which the different approaches further, or limit, the advancement of gender equality.

4.1 *The Scope of 'Sex'*

'Sex' as a ground of discrimination could be limited to discrimination based on biological differences, but in both the international and the domestic legal contexts it has not been so narrowly defined. 'Sex' was quickly broadened to explicitly include gender by the *CEDAW* Committee,[648] and while the HRC and the CESCR do not explicitly state that discrimination on the grounds of sex includes gender, most of the sex discrimination decisions of the HRC are instances of gender discrimination. For example, the *Mauritius* case focused on law that presumed women were dependent on men and would upon marriage move to their husband's country, both differences grounded in gender.[649] The *Avellanal* case focused on legislation which denied married women the right to pursue an action before the courts. The legislation reflects gender differences, rather than sex differences, including that upon marriage a husband and wife are one person in law so that 'the very being or legal existence of the woman is incorporated or consolidated into that of her husband, under whose wing, protection and cover, she performs everything'[650] and that women are 'not able to protect themselves against those who might take advantage of their lack of knowledge and judgement.'[651] The extension of the scope of sex to include gender is not explicitly expressed in the legislation of the three country examples, however, as with the HRC cases, sex discrimination claims primarily rest on gender differences. For example, in the United States in *Phillips*

648 *General Recommendation 28*, above n. 140, at paras 3, 5, 16, 17; and *General Recommendation 25*, UN Doc A/59/38, annex I, at paras 5, 7 and 11.

649 Frances Raday, 'Gender and Democratic Citizenship: The Impact of CEDAW' *International Journal of Constitutional Law* 10(2) (2012), 512–530: 522.

650 William Blackstone, *Commentaries on the Laws of England* Volume 1 (Oxford: Clarendon Press, 1765–1769), Chapter 15, at para 4.

651 Marsha Freeman, 'The Human Rights of Women in the Family: Issues and Recommendations for the Implementation of the Women's Convention' in Julie Peters and Andrea Wolper (eds.), *Women's Rights, Human Rights: International Feminist Perspectives* (London: Routledge, 1995), 149–157: 151.

the defendant refused to hire mothers with young children and in *Dothard* a prison refused to hire female guards because their 'womanhood' would undermine security. In Australia in *Ho* a female employee was ordered to change the towels in the men's bathroom and in *Zhang* a female was required to wear a mini skirt in the gaming room in which she worked. In India in *R.S Singh*, like in *Dothard*, a prison refused to hire female prison guards because of a perception they would be unable to control male inmates and in *Rani Raj* females were declared unfit to manage their estates because of their perceived incapacity to deal with legal financial matters. All these cases involve gender differences and not sex differences.

Beyond gender there have been further expansions to the scope of sex in the international context. According to all three treaty-bodies, violence against women is a form of sex discrimination. The *ICESCR* explicitly states in General Comment No. 16 that 'gender-based violence is a form of discrimination that inhibits the ability to enjoy rights and freedoms, including economic, social and cultural rights, on a basis of equality'; the HRC states in *M.T.* that the gang rape and the non-consensual sterilization suffered by the victim constitutes sex discrimination in violation of Article 26, and the *CEDAW* Committee has confirmed in Views and concluding observations that violence against women is sex discrimination under Article 1. Other expansions of the scope of sex in the international law context include a determination by the HRC that sex includes sexual orientation and that the denial of abortion services is a sex-related restriction. The *CESRC* has expanded sex to include pregnancy while the *CEDAW* Committee has expanded the scope of sex to include any reproductive characteristics.[652]

In the three country examples there have been expansions to the meaning of sex. In the United States sex includes pregnancy but not breast-feeding.[653] In India the scope of sex has been recently expanded to include sexual orientation and in the United States to same-sex and transgender status. In Australia there is separate protection from discrimination on the ground of pregnancy, gender identity and sexual orientation so there has been no impetus or reason to extend the scope of sex to include these further characteristics.

652 Loveday Hodson, 'Women's Rights and the Periphery: CEDAW's Optional Protocol' *European Journal of International Law* 25(2) (2014), 561–578.

653 Sheerine Alemzadeh, 'Claiming Disability, Reclaiming Pregnancy: A Critical Analysis of the ADA's Pregnancy Exclusion' *Wisconsin Journal of Law Gender and Society* 27 (2012), 1–37: 7; and Ashley Alteri, 'Gender-Based Discrimination in the Workplace: Why Courts Tell Employers That Breastfeeding Discrimination Is Legal' *Review of Public Personnel Administration* 36(3) (2016), 264–282.

Although there is considerable inconsistency in the scope of sex across the different jurisdictions there are, conversely, striking similarities in the ways in which women experience sex discrimination which are clearly illustrated by the cases. In all jurisdictions, the cases reveal that women experience sex discrimination in similar forms, including gender-based violence and sexual harassment, discrimination in the workplace on the basis of pregnancy and pregnancy-related events such as breast-feeding, and returns from maternity leave resulting in dismissals or demotions. Although women are experiencing similar forms of sex discrimination, their access to the protection of the law varies depending on the scope of sex in the jurisdictions in which they live.

4.2 *The Requirement of an 'Individual' Victim*

In both the international and domestic law contexts, sex discrimination claims must be brought by persons who are themselves victims of sex discrimination or in some limited circumstances by others on their behalf, which limits the capacity of the law to address the structural disadvantages that women face. In international human rights law, a 'legitimate' victim is required for a sex discrimination communication to move through to assessment on its merits under the relevant Optional Protocols to the *ICCPR*, *ICESCR* and *CEDAW*.[654] A communication can be submitted under the Optional Protocols to the *ICESCR* and the *CEDAW* Committee 'by or on behalf of individuals or groups of individuals, under the jurisdiction of a State Party, claiming to be victims of a violation of any of the ...rights set forth in the Covenant'[655] and to the HRC by the 'individuals who claim that any of their rights enumerated in the Covenant have been violated.'[656]

The requirement for an individual victim has led to the exclusion of communications by both the HRC and the *CEDAW* Committee on the basis that the authors are not victims within the meaning of their respective Optional Protocols. For example, the HRC excluded claims of most of the authors in the *Mauritian Women Case* because they were not themselves married to non-nationals. It was insufficient that the law removed their prospective right

654 Optional Protocol to the International Covenant on Civil and Political Rights 23 March 1976; Optional Protocol to the International Covenant on Economic, Social and Cultural Rights A/RES/63/117, 10 December 2008; and Optional Protocol to the Convention on the Elimination of All Forms of Discrimination against Women A/RES/54/4 15 October 1999.

655 Optional Protocol to the International Covenant on Economic, Social and Cultural Rights 2008, Article 2; and Optional Protocol to the Convention on the Elimination of All Forms of Discrimination against Women 1999, Article 2.

656 Optional Protocol to the International Covenant on Civil and Political Rights 1976, Article 2.

to equality in citizenship and might impact on the marriage choices they made in the future. The HRC stated: 'If the law or practice has not already been concretely applied to the detriment of that individual, it must in any event be applicable in such a way that the alleged victim's risk of being affected is more than a theoretical possibility.'[657] In an example from the *CEDAW* Committee, a Philippines national married to a Denmark national went through a gruelling two-year process to regain custody of her son after her husband did not return her son to her after a visitation.[658] She eventually did win custody of her son, returned to the Philippines and lodged an individual complaint basing her victim status on two grounds. Firstly, because she did not have sole custody of the child, she argued she may be subjected to the same ordeal if she returned to Denmark; and secondly, because she was determined that 'what happened to her should not happen to other foreign women married to Danish nationals.'[659] The Committee declared her communication inadmissible on both grounds. The Committee found that she ceased being a victim when she was awarded partial custody of her child because 'they are both living happily in the Philippines and …her son is maintaining contact with his father through the internet.'[660] She can claim sole custody, the Committee found, without going back to Denmark.[661] Additionally, Article 2 of the Optional Protocol excludes communications on behalf of groups of individuals without their prior consent, unless the absence of consent can be justified. The Committee resolved that author did not address the question of consent of the 'other foreign women married to Danish nationals'[662] and therefore it determined that it could not consider the present communication for the sake of 'other foreign women married to Danish nationals.'[663]

There are two important reasons why the narrow reading and understanding of victim by the HRC and the *CEDAW* Committee may not be in accord with their own definitions of sex discrimination. Firstly, Article 1 *CEDAW*, and the HRC in General Comment No. 18, make clear that discrimination is when a 'distinction, exclusion or restriction' has the 'purpose' or 'effect' of nullifying women's rights. If the purpose of the legislation in the *Mauritius* case is to treat women married to non-nationals differently to men married to non-nationals, based on gender roles and gender stereotypes, then its purpose and

657 *Shirin Aumeeruddy-Cziffra and 19 Other Mauritian Women*, at para 9.2(a).
658 *M.K.D.A.-A v. Denmark* Communication No. 44/2012 CEDAW/C/56/D/44/2012.
659 *Ibid.*, at paras 3, 5.6.
660 *Ibid.*, at para 6.3.
661 *Ibid.*, at para 6.5.
662 *Ibid.*, at para 6.5.
663 *Ibid.*, at para 6.5.

certainly its effect surely extends to every woman with the capacity to marry a non-national. The HRC stated that there must be more than a theoretical possibility of discrimination before a person can be a victim, but this ignores the way in which potential discrimination shapes the choices that women make. Women may choose not to marry non-nationals if it forces them to move to their prospective spouse's country of residence; women may choose not to work for an employer with discriminatory work conditions; same-sex women may choose not to teach in a school that has the legislative capacity to dismiss same-sex teachers. Secondly, *CEDAW* explicitly identifies substantive equality as a primary objective of the convention. Article 2(a) *CEDAW* requires states parties to 'embody the principle of the equality of men and women in their national constitutions or other appropriate legislation if not yet incorporated therein and to ensure, through law and other appropriate means, the practical realisation of this principle.' In the case examples discussed above, the denial of victim status appears contrary to the objective of achieving substantive equality. For example, refusing to consider sex discrimination facing non-national women in Denmark because the author does not (and cannot) obtain consent from other potential victims despite the obvious and certain presence of the discriminatory law clearly frustrates the substantive equality objective of *CEDAW*.[664]

In the three country examples, similarly, a person must be a victim of sex discrimination to bring a claim and if there is no victim the discriminatory law or policy can continue without violating sex discrimination law. This narrow perspective means, as illustrated in many of the cases, that women who are deterred from applying to work in a workplace known for employing only men (such as in *Joe's Crabs*), that women who do not pursue job opportunities in workplaces known for sexual harassment, that women who do not join sports clubs with discriminatory policies that deny women equal opportunities to participate cannot bring actions in sex discrimination. These discriminatory practices continue therefore in the absence of victims as defined by the law.

Sex discrimination law, with its requirement for an individual victim, views sex discrimination as a one-off, isolated event, not as a wider problem or a symptom of entrenched policies or practices. This understanding of sex discrimination is reflected in the way the legal system deals with discrimination complaints on a case-by-case basis rather than perceiving it as indicative of a systemic problem. The law assumes that discrimination is a single act

664 Alexandra Harrington, 'Don't Mind the Gap: The Rise of Individual Complaint Mechanisms within International Human Rights Treaties' *Duke Journal of Comparative and International Law* 22 (2011), 153–182: 174.

perpetrated against an individual victim and that it is an unconscious, isolated event rather than a manifestation of entrenched behaviours and practices. There are examples in the international law context, particularly in the work of the *CEDAW* Committee, that provide different approaches that can much more effectively respond to the structural causes of sex discrimination. For example, the findings of the CEDAW Committee in recent inquiries have resulted in recommendations for structural change rather than individual remedies.

4.3 *The Requirement of an Opposite-Sex Comparator*

Direct sex discrimination is prohibited in all jurisdictions – international and domestic – discussed in this volume. Direct sex discrimination claims have been much more successful than indirect sex discrimination claims. However, in most jurisdictions (but not all), the requirement of an opposite-sex comparator in direct sex discrimination claims to determine whether there has been less favourable treatment given to a person on the ground of sex has reduced successful outcomes to those that are the most straightforward and overt cases of discrimination.

In the three treaty-bodies examined in the volume, an opposite-sex comparator is regularly deployed only by the HRC. The HRC has understood the definition in General Comment No. 18 of a 'distinction, exclusion, restriction or preference' based on sex to mean that there must be a comparison between similarly-situated men and women and differentiation found before there can be sex discrimination. Although the opposite-sex comparator approach has provided women some success in sex discrimination claims in the HRC it has also led to some disappointing in outcomes. In *Vos,* for example, the plaintiff failed because there was no opposite-sex comparator, despite the obvious sex discrimination she experienced. If the HRC had not required an opposite-sex comparator or had compared a disabled widow author with a hypothetical disabled woman who is not a widow, then they would have identified sex discrimination.

The *CESCR,* although also requiring an opposite-sex comparator states in General Comment No. 16 that sex discrimination exists when there are 'detrimental acts or omissions on the basis of prohibited grounds' even 'where there is no comparable similar situation (e.g. the case of a woman who is pregnant).'[665] The HRC does not require an opposite-sex comparator in relation to abortion and gender-based violence, however, the dissent of HRC Committee members illustrate how a different outcome would result if they did. Anja Seibert-Fohr reasoned in *Whelan* in relation to abortion:

665 General Comment 20, above n. 138, at para 10(a).

> While it is true that it only affects women, the distinction is explained with a biological difference between women and men that objectively excludes men from the applicability of the law and does not amount to discrimination. Difference in treatment requires comparable situations in order to give rise to discrimination.[666]

Likewise, the argument of a dissenting opinion in *M.T.* was that although the author was the victim of severe violence of a sexual nature, it was not sex discrimination because men could be victims of sexual violence: 'The fact that one individual undergoes such treatment by force is no pointer towards discrimination as such under Article 26.'[667] Although these are dissenting decisions, and the majority HRC did not require an opposite-sex comparator in these instances, these cases illustrate the different outcomes that could result. It enabled the dissenting members to reason that there was no evidence of the victims being treated differently to a similarly-situated male either because there was no similarly-situated male as in *Whelan* or because, as in *M.T.*, a male could also experience sexual violence from the police, if imprisoned, despite statistics indicating the gendered nature of such crimes.

The *CEDAW* Committee, despite Article 1 requiring a 'distinction, exclusion, restriction or preference' based on sex, does not require a similarly-situated opposite-sex comparator and takes a very different approach.[668] Instead of comparing a woman with a similarly-situated male, the *CEDAW* Committee asks if the person has suffered unfavourable treatment because she is a woman. The question is subtly different from a sex neutral or symmetrical anti-discrimination approach focussing on a power imbalance between men and women and resting on a presumption that women are the disproportionate victims of discrimination on the ground of their sex and/or their gender.[669] For example, in considering violence against women, the question asked – is the violence perpetrated because she is a woman – shifts the focus away from a comparison between similarly-situated women and men. In many instances, the question can be answered in the affirmative with support from global statistics that confirm that gender-based harm or discrimination is widespread and perpetrated primarily against women.

---

666 *Whelan*, above n. 100, at para 4.5.

667 *MT*, above n. 92, at para 5 (Dissenting Opinion).

668 Hilary Charlesworth, Christine Chinkin and Shelley Wright, 'Feminist Approaches to International Law' *The American Journal of International Law* 85(4) (1991), 613–645: 631.

669 Rikki Holtmaat, 'The CEDAW: A Holistic Approach to Women's Equality and Freedom' in Anne Hellum and Henriette Sinding Aasen (eds.), *Women's Human Rights: CEDAW in International, Regional and National Law* (Cambridge University Press, 2013), 95–124.

The HRC, although in most instances requiring an opposite-sex comparator as the primary means of identifying direct discrimination, has utilized a same-sex comparator. For example, in the *Mauritian Women Case*, the HRC compared national women married to non-national men with national women married to national men. In *Toonen*, the HRC compared men who have same-sex relations with consenting men in private, with men who have consenting sexual relations with women in private. In *Mellet* and *Whelan*, the HRC, rejecting Ireland's argument that the claim must fail because there is no male comparator, compared women pregnant with a foetus with a fatal impairment (who nevertheless decide to carry the foetus to term) with women pregnant with a foetus with a fatal impairment who choose to travel to terminate the pregnancy in another country. By comparing women with similarly-situated women, the HRC avoided measuring women against a male referent when there is no male referent, as in the case of abortion.[670]

In all three country-examples, successful outcomes have resulted through the use of an opposite-sex comparator but mostly in straightforward cases of direct, explicit discrimination. For example, in Australia, a woman who was denied the opportunity to be a meat slicer, a job exclusively undertaken by men, succeeded through a straightforward comparison with men. In another case, the judge compared the female plaintiff directed to change the towels in the men's washroom with a male employee and found that it was a task that no man would ever be directed to undertake. In a final example, a female member of a Golf Club could not play a full round of golf on Wednesdays and a comparison with male members revealed there was no day in which men could not play a full round of golf.[671] In the United States, in the progressive *Bostock* case, a comparison between a man who could be fired for his relationship with a man when a woman in a relationship with the same man could not, found they were being treated differently on the ground of sex. In India, successful cases resting on an opposite-sex comparator include declaring unlawful a law that declared women unfit to manage their properties, a law that prevented women from working night-shifts in factories and a law that prevented women from working in establishments serving liquor.

670 Katarzyna Sękowska-Kozłowska, 'A Tough Job: Recognizing Access to Abortion as a Matter of Equality. A Commentary on the Views of the UN Human Rights Committee in the Cases of Mellet v. Ireland and Whelan v. Ireland' *Reproductive Health Matters* 26(54) (2018), 25–31: 27; and Lie Weiwei, 'Equality and Non-Discrimination under International Human Rights Law' *Research Notes* 3 (2004), 1–26: 9.

671 Sara Charlesworth, 'The Sex Discrimination Act: Advancing Gender Equality and Decent Work?' in Margaret Thornton (ed.), *Sex Discrimination in Uncertain Times* (ANU E Press, 2010), 133–151: 134.

Despite successful outcomes in all three country-examples where an opposite-sex comparator was successfully deployed, there were also many claims where the lack of an obvious opposite-sex comparator led to failure. Sometimes the lack of an opposite-sex comparator was because of biological difference. For example, in the United States breast-feeding cases have routinely been rejected under Title VII on the basis that there is no male comparator. In India, the courts have characterized gender roles and gender-role stereotypes as inherent (biological) differences between men and women and failed to find opposite-sex comparators. Claims have also failed because the socially constructed roles, behaviours, activities and attributes that a given society assigns to men and women have resulted in no obvious male comparator.[672] For example, in the Australian case of *Zhang*, where the plaintiff was asked to wear a miniskirt, the judge could not find a male comparator.[673]

The limitations of an opposite-sex comparator approach are illustrated in the example cases in this volume, by the commentary of judges themselves,[674] and by academic commentators. The presumption that underscores an opposite-sex comparator approach is that women should be treated like men, if they are similarly situated.[675] However, this means that it is male experience and male perspective that is the benchmark against which women are measured, limiting women to the same opportunities and outcomes as similarly-situated men.[676] For example, women can be meat splicers if they can show themselves as capable as men in utilizing a knife, women can be bus conductors if they meet the physical criteria of men, women can be prison guards if they are able to manage violent offenders as effectively as men. However, if men and women are not or cannot be similarly situated, this approach fails because an opposite-sex comparator requirement is to ensure that likes are treated alike. The assumption underscoring this approach is that once unfair barriers are removed, women can compete fairly. This ignores the fact that women have been historically denied the opportunity to obtain the meritorious characteristics to enable them to compete equally. In addition, sex discrimination

672 Catherine MacKinnon, 'Substantive Equality: A Perspective' *Minnesota Law Review* 96 (2011), 1–28: 5, 13.

673 Simone Cusack and Alexandra S.H. Timmer, 'Gender Stereotyping in Rape Cases: The CEDAW Committee's Decision in Vertido v. The Philippines' *Human Rights Law Review* 11(2) (2011), 329–342.

674 For example, see *Purvis v. New South Wales* (2003) HCA 62, at 114 as per McHugh and Kirby JJ.

675 Dianne Otto, 'Women's Rights' *International Human Rights Law* (2010), 345–364.

676 Martha Fineman, 'The Vulnerable Subject: Anchoring Equality in the Human Condition' in *Transcending the Boundaries of Law* (Routledge-Cavendish, 2010), 177–191.

is viewed as a one-off, isolated event between the individual parties, not as a complex web of entrenched practices.[677]

In contrast, the substantive equality approach taken by the CEDAW Committee, although not unproblematic, removes the need for comparison by instead asking if a person is a member of a persistently disadvantaged group and whether a law, policy, or behaviour maintains or worsens that disadvantage.[678] Although the approach of the CEDAW Committee to sex discrimination is the most likely to be effective at achieving inroads towards substantive equality, it is not yet been adopted by any of the three country-examples. Their approaches therefore do not allow space for the 'deep-seated' reform required to realize substantive gender equality.[679] Objectionable sex-based discriminatory acts, statements, policies and laws occur in the absence of an opposite-sex comparator.[680] Therefore reducing claims to those in which an opposite-sex comparator can be identified leads to important forms of discrimination being missed.[681] Instead, comparators filter out claims rather than enabling the recognition of discrimination and are to be best considered as a useful observational tool rather than an arbiter of whether discrimination can be identified.[682]

4.4 *Indirect Discrimination*

Indirect discrimination has been a difficult avenue for victims to pursue in all jurisdictions discussed in this volume, both international and domestic.[683] All three treaty-bodies require states parties to prohibit indirect sex discrimination.

---

677 Otto, above n. 675, 321.

678 Caroline Lambert, 'Reproducing Discrimination: Promoting the Equal Sharing of Caring Work in CEDAW, at the ILO and in the SDA' in Margaret Thornton (ed.), *Sex Discrimination in Uncertain Times* (ANU E Press, 2010), 153–170: 163.

679 Anne F. Bayefsky, 'The Principle of Equality or Non-Discrimination in International Law' *Human Rights Law Journal* 11 (1990), 1.

680 Suzanne B. Goldberg, 'Discrimination by Comparison' *Yale Law Journal* 120 (2010), 728–814: 733.

681 *Ibid.*, at 735.

682 Goldberg, above n. 680, 742.

683 Beth Gaze, 'The Sex Discrimination Act, at 25: Reflections on the Past, Present and Future' in Margaret Thornton (ed.), *Sex Discrimination in Uncertain Times* (ANU, 2010), 107–132; Kristina Koldinska, 'Case Law of the European Court of Justice on Sex Discrimination 2006–2011' *Common Market Law Review* 48 (2011), 1599; Quynh Vu, 'Reducing the Complainant's Evidentiary Burden of Proving Indirect Sex Discrimination in the Workplace Claim–Easier said than Done?' *New Zealand Journal of Employment Relations (Online)* 44(2) (2020), 74–84; and Sandra Fredman, 'Addressing Disparate Impact: Indirect discrimination and the Public Sector Equality Duty' *Industrial Law Journal* 43(3) (2014), 349–363.

The *CESCR* in particular has provided a comprehensive definition of indirect discrimination in General Comment No. 16 and the HRC has confirmed in a number of its published Views that indirect discrimination is a violation of the *ICCPR*.[684] The *CEDAW* Committee explains in General Recommendation 25(7) that discrimination as it is defined in Article 1 *CEDAW* requires states parties to ensure 'that there is no direct or indirect discrimination against women in their laws.' The Committee reaffirms this in General Recommendation No. 28[685] and has consistently recommended that states parties 'ensure that its national legislation includes a definition of discrimination against women, covering direct and indirect discrimination in the public and private spheres.'[686]

The *CESCR* has had only one opportunity to consider indirect sex discrimination and applied the principle effectively. In the 2018 case of *Marcia Cecilia Trujillo Calero*, the author argued that women experience very different conditions in the workplace than men. In part, the author argued this is because the gendered division of labour, which leaves women responsible for domestic responsibilities and raising children, means they are much more likely to work part-time or work in the home in an unpaid capacity. As a result, their capacity to make payments into a retirement pension, designed around a full-time worker with an uninterrupted working life, may be significantly less than the average male worker. The *CESCR* agreed that the impact of the requirement that contributions be uninterrupted constituted indirect sex discrimination.

The HRC and the *CEDAW* Committee have, however, a mixed record on their ability to identify and remedy indirect sex discrimination. For example, when a law in France prevented women but not men from transmitting their name to their children, the *CEDAW* Committee focused on the fact that the rule applied equally to boys and girls and therefore, they reasoned, since the children were the authors it was not sex discrimination. However, the authors, who wanted to have their mother's names but by law were forced to take their father's names, were surely victims of indirect discrimination. Indeed, the dissenting opinion did view it as indirect discrimination on the basis that the situation the authors found themselves in resulted from legislation that

684 *Simunek et al. v. The Czech Republic Communication* No. 516/1992, Views of 19 July 1995; and *Derksen v. The Netherlands*, Communication No. 976/2001, Views of 1 April 2004.

685 *Ibid.*, at para 16.

686 Concluding Observations of the CEDAW Committee: Cambodia (8 November 2019) 74th Session, at para [9(a)] (UN Doc CEDAW/C/KHM/CO/6). See also similar statements in the Concluding Observations to Kazakhstan (8 November 2019) 74th Session, at para [12(a)] (UN Doc CEDAW/C/KAZ/CO/5); Seychelles (8 November 2019) 74th Session, at para [10(a)] (UN Doc CEDAW/C/SYC/CO/6); and Guyana (30 July 2019) 73th Session, at para [14] (UN Doc CEDAW/C/GUY/CO/9).

clearly discriminated on the ground of sex.[687] Whereas the majority assessed the 'effect' as non-discriminatory because both male and female children were equally affected, the dissent viewed both the 'purpose' and the 'effect' of the rule as discriminatory. The purpose was to enable men but not women to transmit their name and the effect was to prevent children from adopting their mother's name and instead force them to take their father's name. In another case, the law in the Netherlands prevented the author from receiving maternity benefits for both of her part-time jobs. The *CEDAW* Committee named her dual employment status as the reason for her disadvantage and could not perceive the indirect sex discrimination that arose because women disproportionately are employed as part-time workers and are much more likely to be juggling two jobs than men. The Committee's narrow approach highlights the limits of sex discrimination law in cases of indirect discrimination.

In all the country-examples, indirect discrimination claims have had limited success. In India indirect sex discrimination is not explicitly recognized and is not a viable avenue for sex discrimination claims. While indirect discrimination is explicitly recognized in Title VII and the SDA, claims in both Australia and the United States, as in the international context, have had limited success. For example, in the United States, clearly discriminatory hiring practices over many years resulting in all-male food servers in a popular restaurant did not satisfy the indirect sex discrimination requirements because women simply did not apply for jobs they knew they would not get.[688] In Australia, although there have been a greater number of successful cases, they are still limited.

The examples in this volume illustrate that indirect sex discrimination is rarely identified and remedied within the legal structures as they are currently framed in both the international and domestic contexts. Indirect discrimination is more difficult to identify[689] as its neutral façade can make the effects less obvious and the measures which result in the discriminatory effect less easy to detect.[690] However, indirect discrimination often fosters and perpetuates broad structural inequalities so the failure of sex discrimination processes

687 Dubravka Šimonović, Yoko Hayashi, Ruth Halperin-Kaddari, Silvia Pimentel, Violeta Neubauer and Saisuree Chutikul.

688 David Sherwyn, Melenie J. Lankau, and Zev Eigen, 'The Good, the Bad, and the Ugly: The Peculiar Discrimination Case of Joe's Stone Crabs' *The Cornell Hotel and Restaurant Administration Quarterly* 40(5) (1999), 10–17: 15, 17.

689 Bistra Netkova, 'Gender and the Right to Non-Discrimination in International Human Rights Law' *Journal of Liberty and International Affairs* 3(1) (2016), 20–30: 25, 27.

690 Sophia Moreau, 'The Moral Seriousness of Indirect Discrimination' in Hugh Collins and Tarunabh Khaitan (eds.), *Foundations of Indirect Discrimination Law* (Hart Publishing, 2018), 123–149: 128.

to recognize and remedy indirect discrimination is a significant failing in sex discrimination law.[691]

4.5 *The Requirement of an Intent to Discriminate*

Intent to discriminate is not a required element of establishing sex discrimination, direct or indirect, in the jurisprudence of the HRC, the *CESCR* and the *CEDAW* Committee. Article 1 *CEDAW* states that the term 'discrimination against women' shall mean any distinction, exclusion or restriction made on the basis of sex which has the effect or purpose of impairing or nullifying the recognition, enjoyment or exercise by women, irrespective of their marital status, on a basis of equality of men and women, of human rights and fundamental freedoms in the political, economic, social, cultural, civil or any other field. General Recommendation 28 of the *CEDAW* Committee explains that the phrase 'effect or purpose' means that it can be sex discrimination 'even where discrimination was not intended.' This makes clear that intent is not relevant to determining sex discrimination in the eyes of the *CEDAW* Committee.[692] In the Views published by the HRC and the *CEDAW* Committee (and in the single sex discrimination complaint heard by the *CESCR*), intent is not referred to and does not appear as a requirement, whether the complaint relates to direct or indirect discrimination. In one exception, the HRC appeared to place weight on the beneficial intent of legislation in finding that there was no sex discrimination. Although this is a case of an intent not to discriminate, rather than an intent to discriminate, the underlying presumption is similar. A positive intent of legislation, in our view, should not be relevant to the sex discrimination experienced by the victim.

Although intent is not required in direct sex discrimination claims under section 15(1) of the Indian Constitution or direct and indirect sex discrimination claims under s. 5 of the SDA, intent to discriminate on the ground of sex is required for disparate treatment claims (but not disparate impact claims) under Title VII in the United States. This has led to the failure of claims that might otherwise succeed[693] and has also led to the view that direct

691 Tarunabh Khaitan and Sandy Steele, 'Wrongs, Group Advantage and the Legitimacy of Indirect Discrimination Law' in Hugh Collins and Tarunabh Khaitan (eds.), *Foundations of Indirect Discrimination Law* (Hart Publishing, 2018), 199, 200.

692 Bistra Netkova, 'Gender and the Right to Non-discrimination in International Human Rights Law' *Journal of Liberty and International Affairs* 1(3) (2016), 20–29: 25.

693 Sandra Fredman, 'Direct and Indirect 'Discrimination: Is there Still a Divide?' in Hugh Collins and Tarunabh Khaitan (eds.), *Foundations of Indirect Discrimination Law* (Hart Publishing, 2018), 31–57.

discrimination is more 'culpable' than indirect discrimination.[694] The role of intent is not clearly explained in the United States cases but appears to be based on a perception of unfairness or injustice in awarding compensation based on motivations of which the decision maker is unaware.[695]

However, while a requirement for intent in the criminal law, for example, which focuses upon the state of mind of the accused as the central organizing mechanism for assessing crimes and assigning levels of punishment, the aims of discrimination law are different.[696] It is unclear why, if the defendant is 'indifferent', 'mistaken' or basing a decision on 'stereotypes and generalizations', no sex discrimination should be found.[697] For example, an employer may genuinely believe that a mother is less able to perform her job than a woman without children and it is unclear why this should be differentiated from an employer who intentionally sets out to exclude mothers. The discriminatory effect on the victim is the primary concern. Indeed, the primary goal of anti-discrimination legislation is to prevent and end discrimination and to provide remedies for victims.[698] Additionally, discriminators are unlikely to admit discriminatory intent[699] and workplaces and other institutions can obscure intent by embedding structural disadvantages that are not easily traced to a particular practice or policy.[700]

4.6 *Multiple Discrimination*

Multiple discrimination, intersectionality, has been recognized by all three treaty-bodies as violating their respective conventions. The CEDAW Committee, in particular, has highlighted the negative and cumulative effects of multiple discrimination on women in its concluding observations and general

694 Sophia Moreau, 'The Moral Seriousness of Indirect Discrimination' in Hugh Collins and Tarunabh Khaitan (eds.), *Foundations of Indirect Discrimination Law* (Hart Publishing, 2018) 123–148.

695 Leora F. Eisenstadt and Jeffrey R. Boles, 'Intent and Liability in Employment' *American Business Law Journal* 43(4) (2016), 607–675: 610.

696 *Ibid.*, at 639.

697 Don Welch, 'Removing Discriminatory Barriers: Basing Disparate Treatment Analysis on Motive Rather Than Intent' *Southern California Law Review* 60(733) (1987), 734–782: 744.

698 Amelia M. Wirts, 'Discriminatory Intent and Implicit Bias: Title VII Liability for Unwitting Discrimination' *Boston College Law Review* 58(2) (2017), 809–856: 815; and Goldberg, above n. 680, 740.

699 Goldberg, above n. 680, at 731; and Aziz Huq, 'What Is Discriminatory Intent' *Cornell Law Review* 103 (2017), 1211.

700 Goldberg, above n. 680, 737.

recommendations.[701] Despite this, both the HRC and the *CEDAW* Committee have struggled to recognize and acknowledge multiple discrimination and its compounding impact on victims in their published Views.

In the *Mauritius* case, for example, the HRC reduced the discrimination experienced by the victims on the basis of both marital status and sex, to sex discrimination.[702] In *L.N.P. v. Argentina,* where a 15-year-old girl, P from a marginalized ethnic minority group (the Qom) in Argentina, was sexually assaulted by three men, the HRC, although finding for the author, did not acknowledge the obvious multiple discriminations at play which clearly exacerbated the harm to the victim. It did not increase the compensation it recommended to reflect the multiple discriminations. The *CEDAW* Committee also has failed in some instances to recognize multiple discriminations. For example, in *Kayhan*, the author was dismissed for wearing a headscarf and claimed religious persecution and violation of her right to work. In *Zheng* the author was a victim of sex trafficking but did not use a sex discrimination avenue in her domestic proceedings. In both examples the authors were victims of multiple discriminations including sex but both claims were found inadmissible on the basis that the authors did not explicitly identify sex discrimination in their domestic proceedings. Yet the authors' reasons for not utilizing sex discrimination were that the domestic law required a single ground of discrimination to be identified. For example, in *Kayhan* the domestic regulations which prohibited headscarfs and gave rise to her claim of discrimination were gender neutral, yet it is women who wear headscarfs. The plaintiff had to choose between religious discrimination or sex discrimination, rather than relying on the compounded impact of both, and chose the avenue most likely to succeed.[703] In addition, many women who face multiple and intersecting discrimination may find it difficult to determine the precise origin of the unfavourable treatment, particularly indirect sex discrimination, which is often disguised in seemingly neutral laws and policies. Sex discrimination can be a difficult avenue to pursue successfully in the domestic legal context and the remedies often

701 Concluding Observations of the *CEDAW* Committee: Pakistan 75th Session, at para 14(b) March 2020 (UN Doc CEDAW/C/PAK/CO/5); and Concluding Observations of the *CEDAW* Committee: Bulgaria 75th Session, at para 10 March 2020 (UN Doc CEDAW/C/BGR/CO/8). Concluding Observations of the *CEDAW* Committee: Republic of Moldova 75th Session, at para 11 March 2020 (UN Doc CEDAW/C/MDA/CO/6).

702 Shreya Atrey, 'Fifty Years On: The Curious Case of Intersectional Discrimination in the ICCPR' *Nordic Journal of Human Rights* 35(3) (2017), 220–239.

703 Heiner Bielefeldt, Nazila Ghanea-Hercock, and Michael Wiener, *Freedom of Religion or Belief: An International Law Commentary* (Oxford University Press, 2016).

inadequate. Strategically then, in the domestic context where the stakes are much more immediate, contextual, and the outcome of significant immediate importance raising sex discrimination may not be the most appropriate or effective avenue.

The CEDAW Committee has in some cases recognized the complexities of multiple discrimination.[704] In *Pimentel*, the Committee identified the intersection of sex and indigeneity when an Afro-Brazilian woman died of complications resulting from her pregnancy. They identified the uneven distribution of higher-level health facilities across the country as connected to her status as an indigenous person and as a woman. In *Kell*, where the author was victim of domestic violence and lost her home, the Committee similarly recognized the compounding effect of both the author's indigeneity and her gender. In *R.P.* where a 17-year-old, deaf and mute girl was raped by her 19-year-old neighbour in her own residence, her vulnerability as a deaf and mute girl was noted in the Views and recommendations of the Committee. Finally, the recent inquiry into violence against Aboriginal women and girls in Canada indicated an in-depth understanding of how the intersection of gender and indigeneity heightened their vulnerability to violence and heightened the consequences for them.[705] The Committee appears more equipped to recognize discrimination when it manifests in more obvious ways and is less able when it is more nuanced and complex.[706]

Australia, the United States and India have not translated the international obligation to recognize multiple discrimination into their domestic legislative frameworks. All three countries have legal frameworks that explicitly separate the grounds of discrimination into discrete categories and there is no provision for the recognition of multiple discriminations. A person who has experienced multiple discriminations must choose one of the protected grounds of discrimination on which to base their claim. In India not only are multiple discriminations not recognized but the interpretation of Article 15(1) of the Indian Constitution has meant, until very recently that if there are multiple grounds of discrimination there can be no sex discrimination at all. This is because Article 15(1) has been interpreted to mean that sex discrimination can only be found if it is the sole cause of discrimination. For example, the court did not find sex discrimination when a petitioner was discriminated against on

704 Hodson, above n. 652, at 570.

705 Rebecca Cook and Simone Cusack, 'The Committee on the Elimination of Discrimination against Women' (Edward Elgar Publishing Ltd., 2018), 23.

706 Emily Gabos, 'The Intersectionality of the Committee on the Elimination of Discrimination against Women' *MUNDI* 1(1) (2020), 1–48.

the basis of both property ownership discrimination and sex and in another example on the basis that women were denied the opportunity to be shed clerks not only because of their sex but also because of their physical structure and susceptibilities.

The failure to recognize the compounding impact of additional discriminations on victims of sex discrimination is a significant failing in both the international law context and the three country-examples set out in this volume.[707] Multiple discrimination may magnify the harms experienced.[708] This is relevant in a practical sense to sanctions and remedies but it is also symbolically important to the recognition of the magnitude of the infringement of the right or the harm suffered.[709] Finally and importantly, a failure to recognize multiple discrimination limits the capacity of sex discrimination law to address the structural sources of inequality. Individuals are often targeted by discriminators because of their identity as a whole rather than one particular trait such as sex.[710] However, the structure of sex discrimination law means that it cannot recognize the reality of multiple discrimination and as a result, 'courts have basically given up on the complex subject.'[711]

4.7 *Concluding Comments*

Sex discrimination claims are a limited means of addressing the structural inequalities experienced by women. This volume has illustrated that the

---

707 Eric Grollman, 'Multiple Disadvantaged Statuses and Health: The Role of Multiple Forms of Discrimination' *Journal of Health and Social Behavior* 55(1) (2014), 3–19; Jim Sidanius and Rosemary C. Veniegas, 'Gender and Race Discrimination: The Interactive Nature of Disadvantage' in *Reducing Prejudice and Discrimination* (Psychology Press, 2013), 57–80; and Leah R. Warner and Stephanie A. Shields, 'The Intersections of Sexuality, Gender, and Race: Identity Research, at the Crossroads' *Sex Roles* 68(11–12) (2013), 803–810.

708 Trino Grillo, 'Anti-Essentialism and Intersectionality: Tools to Dismantle the Master's House' Berkeley Women's Law Journal 10 (1995), 16–30; Archana Parashar, 'Essentialism or Pluralism: the Future of Legal Feminism' *Canadian Journal of Women and the Law* 6 (1993), 328–348; Mari Matsuda, 'Pragmatism Modified and the False Consciousness Problem' *Southern Californian Law Review* 63 (1990), 1763–1782; Angela Harris, 'Race and Essentialism in Feminist Legal Theory' *Stanford Law Review* 42 (1990), 581–616; and Kimberley Crenshaw, 'Demarginalizing the Intersection of Race and Sex: A Black Critique of Anti-Discrimination Doctrine, Feminist Theory and Anti-Racist Politics' *University of Chicago Legal Forum* (1989), 139–167.

709 Rachel Kahn Best, Lauren Edelman, Linda Krieger and Scott Ellison, 'Multiple Disadvantages: An Empirical Test of Intersectionality Theory in EEO Litigation' *Law & Society Review* 45(4) (2011), 991–1025.

710 Goldberg, above n. 680, 736.

711 Minna Kotkin, 'Diversity and Discrimination: A Look, at Complex Bias' *William and Mary Law Review* 50 (2009), 1439, 1462.

international law approach to sex discrimination by treaty-bodies is more progressive, flexible and wide-reaching than in the three country examples. Indeed, in all three country examples the standards set by the treaty-bodies have not been translated into law in large part. Instead, sex discrimination claims in all three countries are governed by inflexible rules including requirements for opposite-sex comparators, causation requirements that exclude obvious examples of sex discrimination, an intent to discriminate and defences that enable those who discriminate to argue a business justification for their conduct. The result is that while straightforward examples of formal inequality can be rectified through this framework, more complex and structural examples of sex discrimination cannot.

Despite the different social, political, and cultural contexts of the three country-examples and the wide-ranging context of the communications heard by the treaty-bodies from every region of the world, the similarities in the sex discrimination experienced by women is notable. In all countries women were victims of gender-based violence and sexual harassment, in all countries women were discriminated against by airlines who treated them less favourably than men on the basis of marriage pregnancy and age, and in all countries there were examples of women's employment being terminated on the basis of pregnancy or upon their return to work from maternity leave.

There were also examples in all three country-examples of men claiming sex discrimination and, in most instances, utilizing the law to claim rights that had been awarded to women in recognition of historical disadvantage. Some opportunities are provided in the HRC and in some domestic contexts to defend sex discrimination for 'reasonable' business reasons. Reasonableness as a standard for behaviour, and in some circumstances as a defence, is common in many areas of law and allows decision-makers to rest on their own subjectivity. If the discriminator can convince the decision-maker that there is a reasonable justification for her or his actions, despite the impact on the victim, it will not constitute sex discrimination. Like the requirement for intent, if the overarching aim of sex discrimination law is to prevent sex discrimination, to provide relief for victims and to support structural reform, these avenues of escaping responsibility appear counter-productive.

The work that sex discrimination law does ultimately appears to be limited.

www.ingramcontent.com/pod-product-compliance
Lightning Source LLC
LaVergne TN
LVHW102228300926
849160LV00005B/62